THE LEGEND of
ALBERT
TROSTEL
& SONS

THE LEGEND of ALBERT TROSTEL & SONS

JEFFREY L. RODENGEN
RICHARD F. HUBBARD

Edited by Jon VanZile and Torey Marcus
Design and layout by Sandy Cruz

Write Stuff Enterprises, Inc.
1001 South Andrews Avenue
Second Floor
Fort Lauderdale, FL 33316
1-800-900-Book (1-800-900-2665)
(954) 462-6657
www.writestuffbooks.com

Publisher's Cataloging in Publication

Hubbard, Richard F.
    The legend of Albert Trostel & Sons/
Richard F. Hubbard & Jeffrey L. Rodengen;
edited by Jon VanZile and Torey Marcus;
design and layout by Sandy Cruz. — 1st ed.
    p. cm.
    Includes bibliographical references and index.

    LCCN 2002111017
    ISBN 0-945903-97-9

    1. Albert Trostel & Sons. 2. Leather industry
and trade — United States. 3. Automobile
supplies industry — United States. I.
Rodengen, Jeffrey L. II. VanZile, Jon III.
Marcus, Torey. IV. Title

HD9780.U54A43 2004   338.4'7685'0973
                          QBI04-200171

Completely produced in the
United States of America
10 9 8 7 6 5 4 3 2 1

Also by Jeffrey L. Rodengen

The Legend of Chris-Craft

IRON FIST:
The Lives of Carl Kiekhaefer

Evinrude-Johnson
and The Legend of OMC

Serving the Silent Service:
The Legend of Electric Boat

The Legend of Dr Pepper/Seven-Up

The Legend of Honeywell

The Legend of Briggs & Stratton

The Legend of Ingersoll-Rand

The Legend of Stanley:
150 Years of The Stanley Works

The MicroAge Way

The Legend of Halliburton

The Legend of York International

The Legend of Nucor Corporation

The Legend of Goodyear:
The First 100 Years

The Legend of AMP

The Legend of Cessna

The Legend of VF Corporation

The Spirit of AMD

The Legend of Rowan

New Horizons:
The Story of Ashland Inc.

The History of American Standard

The Legend of Mercury Marine

The Legend of Federal-Mogul

Against the Odds:
Inter-Tel—The First 30 Years

The Legend of Pfizer

State of the Heart:
The Practical Guide to Your Heart
and Heart Surgery
with Larry W. Stephenson, M.D.

The Legend of
Worthington Industries

The Legend of IBP, Inc.

The Legend of
Trinity Industries, Inc.

The Legend of
Cornelius Vanderbilt Whitney

The Legend of Amdahl

The Legend of Litton Industries

The Legend of Gulfstream

The Legend of Bertram
with David A. Patten

The Legend of
Ritchie Bros. Auctioneers

The Legend of ALLTEL
with David A. Patten

The Yes, you can of
Invacare Corporation
with Anthony L. Wall

The Ship in the Balloon:
The Story of Boston Scientific
and the Development of
Less-Invasive Medicine

The Legend of Day & Zimmermann

The Legend of Noble Drilling

Fifty Years of Innovation:
Kulicke & Soffa

Biomet—From Warsaw
to the World
with Richard F. Hubbard

NRA: An American Legend

The Heritage and Values
of RPM, Inc.

The Marmon Group:
The First Fifty Years

The Legend of Grainger

The Legend of
The Titan Corporation
with Richard F. Hubbard

The Legend of Discount Tire Co.
with Richard F. Hubbard

The Legend of Polaris
with Richard F. Hubbard

The Legend of La-Z-Boy
with Richard F. Hubbard

The Legend of McCarthy
with Richard F. Hubbard

InterVoice:
Twenty Years of Innovation
with Richard F. Hubbard

Jefferson-Pilot Financial:
A Century of Excellence
with Richard F. Hubbard

The Legend of HCA
with Richard F. Hubbard

The Legend of Werner Enterprises
with Richard F. Hubbard

The History of J. F. Shea Co.
with Richard F. Hubbard

True to Our Vision
with Richard F. Hubbard

TABLE OF CONTENTS

Introduction vi

Acknowledgments viii

Chapter I   Origins: Milwaukee and Germany 10

Chapter II   The Tannery 18

Chapter III   Changing of the Guard 30

Chapter IV   The Depression and Its Aftermath 38

Chapter V   World War II 46

Chapter VI   Postwar Diversification 54

Chapter VII   The End of an Era 70

Chapter VIII   Focus, Focus, Focus! 82

Chapter IX   New Leadership in a Decade of Globalization 96

Chapter X   The Dawn of a New Millennium 112

Appendix A   The Trostel Family Tree 126

Appendix B   The Trostel & Sons Organizational Chart 127

Notes to Sources 128

Index 136

INTRODUCTION

PEOPLE HAVE BEEN PRO-cessing leather long before recorded history. At nearly a century and a half, the leather legacy of Albert Trostel & Sons is among the most impressive of the 20th and 21st centuries. Since its inception, this Milwaukee-based company has been refining the very art of leather processing.

The Albert Trostel & Sons story begins with the arrival of Albert Gottlieb Trostel in mid-19th-century Milwaukee, Wisconsin. The 18-year-old emigrated from Germany to the burgeoning Midwestern city in 1852 with barely a penny in his pocket, yet he arrived as a well-trained and skilled craftsman.

In 1858, Trostel formed a partnership and leased a leather tannery with his friend August Gallun. Soon after Trostel and Gallun joined forces, the Civil War broke out, creating an enormous demand for leather to make boots and countless items for horse-drawn transportation. Trostel and Gallun were well on their way to distinguishing their tannery from a glut of opportunistic competitors that had sprung up throughout Milwaukee.

But leather is only part of the Albert Trostel & Sons story. There is a Chinese proverb that implores those who are too set in their ways to "adapt yourself to changing circumstances." Considering the vast changes in our society since 1858, it shouldn't come as a surprise that this unique company has become very adept at the fine art of adaptation.

The executives who have guided Albert Trostel & Sons throughout the past century and a half—Albert Gottlieb Trostel, his son Gustav Trostel, Albert Gottlieb's grandson Albert O. Trostel Jr., Everett Smith, Anders Segerdahl, and Randy Perry—may have been of German and other European ancestries, but they have flourished in the promise of the American dream. Their perseverance, flexibility, and entrepreneurial spirit in the face of ever-changing industry have determined the company's direction since its earliest days.

In fact, it was another war that underscored the company's ability to adapt. Albert Trostel & Sons was required to diversify its product lines during World War II, manufacturing leather seals and gaskets for military machinery and vehicles in the 1940s. When the war was over, Albert O. Trostel Jr. noted that not only did the products create revenue for the company, but they had become staples of its product line. With mechanical leather clearly part of Trostel's future, the Leather Packings Division was formed in 1946.

Product development became something of a company mandate under Albert O. Trostel Jr.'s leadership, and the company soon moved from leather seals to synthetic seals to urethane seals, and finally to thermoplastic components. Changing with the advent of new technologies ensured the company's continued success, especially during the 1960s when competition from overseas cut into the company's shoe-leather business, forcing Albert Trostel & Sons to close its Milwaukee tannery. But it never lost sight of leather—1961 saw Trostel purchase Eagle Ottawa, a Michigan-based tanner that specialized in automobile and furniture upholstery.

Time and again, diversification paid off for Albert Trostel & Sons. Today, Eagle Ottawa is one of three Trostel subsidiaries. The other two—Trostel Ltd. (rubber) and Trostel SEG (plastics)—are vital legacies of the Leather Packings Division that have taken Albert Trostel & Sons far from the realm of its leather origins.

Throughout all this change, Trostel's leaders have remained steadfast in the company's philosophy and culture. For 146 years, Trostel has been privately held, which has enabled decision makers to invest in the long term. Furthermore, its three subsidiaries continue to foster an entrepreneurial spirit among a talented leadership team and workforce. Finally, there is the company's unwavering devotion to its customers, which has always driven adaptation and continuous quality improvement throughout the organization.

Though change has been a tradition at Albert Trostel & Sons for many generations, its unwavering commitment to its customers, employees, and the quality of its diverse products has produced a truly legendary company.

ACKNOWLEDGMENTS

MANY DEDICATED PEOPLE ASSISTED IN the research, preparation, and publication of *The Legend of Albert Trostel & Sons.*

The principal research and assembly of the narrative time line was accomplished by research assistant Karen Ehrle. Executive editor Torey Marcus and former executive editor Jon VanZile oversaw the text and photos from beginning to end, and the graphic design of Senior Art Director Sandy Cruz brought the story to life.

A number of key people associated with Albert Trostel & Sons lent their efforts to the book's completion, sharing their experiences, providing valuable oversight for accuracy, and helping guide the book's development from outline to final form: Anders Segerdahl, chairman and CEO; Randy Perry, president and COO; Charles Krull, retired vice president and CFO; Tom Hauske Jr., treasurer; and Lee Cook, executive administrator.

Many other executives, employees, retirees, and family members enriched the book by discussing their experiences. The authors extend particular gratitude to these men and women for their candid recollections and guidance: Tim Baker, Bruce Betters, Helmut Beutel, Neil Dunn, DeWayne Egly, Frank Fermano, Bob Gamache, Julian Hatton Jr., Charlie Hicks, Joyce Huck, Merrill Karcher, Robert Kasten, Michael Kirst, Charles Koch, Ellen Ludwig, Thomas Mahnke, Pat Oldenkamp, Jim Orth, Patrick Roeser, Nancy Schlicher, Thomas Sloane, Jerry Sumpter, Craig Tonti, Albert O. Trostel III, and Kevin Velik.

Special thanks are extended to the dedicated staff and associates at Write Stuff Enterprises,

Inc.: Peter Donald, Debra Kronowitz, and Mickey Murphy, senior editors; Kevin Allen, copy editor; Rachelle Donley and Dennis Shockley, art directors; Mary Aaron, transcriptionist; Barbara Koch, indexer; Bruce Borich, production manager; Marianne Roberts, vice president of administration; Sherry Hasso, bookkeeper; Kelly Chapman, executive assistant to Jeffrey L. Rodengen; and Lars Jessen, director of worldwide marketing.

This first painting in Albert Trostel's 100-year commissioned series depicts the tanning process as it begins in the packing house, where the hide is stripped from the carcass. The arcs of the rib cage and musculature set the movement of the painting and are echoed in the folds of the hide, the sweep of the knife, the electrical cable, and the men at work.

CHAPTER ONE

ORIGINS:
MILWAUKEE AND GERMANY

THE BEGINNING—1860

That Milwaukee possesses peculiar advantages for the prosecution of successful manufacturing is a fact so manifest that no argument is needed to establish it. She has an admirable healthful location, a good waterpower, easy water and rail communication, cheap fuel and abundant labor.

—*Milwaukee Sentinel*, January 19, 1874

ON A TREE-LINED STREET IN downtown Milwaukee, just a block from Lake Michigan, lies a modest Italian-style house built in 1872. Amid the series of mid-rise apartment buildings, the cream-colored building could easily be confused for an academic hall or a dean's residence on a sprawling urban campus. Or one might imagine the home handed down among generations of a family that has long resisted development.

The house could be a lot of things to the casual observer. Even most native Milwaukeeans are probably unaware that it serves as headquarters for Albert Trostel & Sons, a diversified producer of plastic, rubber, and leather with $650 million in annual revenues. That the corporate officers of a major global corporation work out of an aging house may seem incongruent, but Albert Trostel & Sons—despite its present size and international scope—has always remained true to its humble origins. The privately held company has been run by strong, grounded leaders who have valued big ideas, reinvestment, and a diligent workforce ever since the tannery was founded by Albert Gottlieb Trostel in 1858.

The roots of Trostel—the man, the company, the principles—can be traced to a family that settled in Germany centuries ago and reared its generations among strong, industrious countrymen who took their work very seriously.[1]

Milwaukee: The Best of Everything

Halfway across the globe, Milwaukee, Wisconsin—the New World setting for the development of Albert Trostel & Sons—was an emerging city that welcomed entrepreneurial men of aspiration, and housed the natural resources necessary for tanning.

To understand Milwaukee's appeal to American tanners, a brief history lesson is in order. The Milwaukee story begins with a geographical development that provided the ideal setting for immigration and industry. Beginning a few million years ago, and until relatively recently (10,000 to 25,000 years ago), great expanses of the Northern Hemisphere were repeatedly buried under seas of ice. Glaciers froze and thawed time after time, kneading the landscape by dredging and mounding the ground, enfolding waterways, and trapping moisture. The power of the ice was so vast that it excavated the Great Lakes, a feat of nature that would help determine the course of commerce within North America.

Albert Trostel emigrated from Germany in 1852 with only his education and skills as an apprentice tanner. He came to Milwaukee and soon founded what would become one of the city's largest tanneries.

An artist's depiction of Milwaukee, showing a surprisingly rugged landscape. The interpretation takes into account dredging and flattening to make way for development, although modern historians think the topography may be exaggerated. *(Milwaukee County Historical Society)*

Fast-forward thousands of years. The presence of white men—fur traders, adventurers, conquerors, explorers, and settlers—in the area later to be named Milwaukee dates to 1795. Progress came rapidly. The city's first election, to choose the delegate to the Michigan Territory's legislative council, took place in the summer of 1835. The following September, Milwaukee men gathered to elect township officers. By 1838, Milwaukee had developed from a trading post to a center of commerce with an entrepreneurial spirit. Boisterous, competitive, hard-drinking, risk-taking individuals—many of them from Trostel's native Germany—in need of work were ready to bank on the opportunities the town offered. In 1846, Milwaukee was incorporated as a city.

By 1848, when Wisconsin became a state, Yankees had begun to settle there in earnest, as it became apparent that the shores of Lake Michigan provided an accessible interior port that promised terrain and climate familiar to immigrating northern Europeans.

Between 1840 and 1850, Milwaukee grew faster than any other American city. It even appeared to be closing the population gap (20,000) with its rival Chicago (27,000), but the lake's commercial advantages shrank in the face of expanding rail travel, and Chicago, a railroad hub, held its lead.[2]

Although it wouldn't be the largest Midwestern city, Milwaukee continued to grow as a commercial center. Everything required for industry, especially the tanning process, was available in abundance. Stockyards in Chicago and Milwaukee provided ample hides, Lake Michigan was a natural and plentiful supplier of water, and forests of oak and hemlock provided the natural tanning agents. Railway and shipping lines were active, so efficient transportation was at hand to bring in supplies and ship out the finished products.[3]

A *Milwaukee Sentinel* article from January 19, 1874, sang the praises of Milwaukee's flourishing industrial setting.

That Milwaukee possesses peculiar advantages for the prosecution of successful manufacturing is a fact so manifest that no argument is needed to establish it. She has an admirable healthful location, a good waterpower, easy water and rail communication, cheap fuel and abundant labor.[4]

The Trostels' Germany

Industry in the new country owed its strength to the knowledgeable and ambitious immigrants who arrived on the nation's shores. Especially in Milwaukee, German immigrants provided a work ethic of precision, dedication, and integrity.

The Trostel family traces its origins to the 15th century and the birth of Andreas Trostel. The family tree indicates that he was born sometime in the 1400s and died in 1522. His only listed heir is Jacobus Trostel, who was probably a grandson. Jacobus lived in Turingen and Andreas in Ossweil, suggesting that the family's roots lie in the Stuttgart region of Germany.

Seven generations later, Georg Michael Trostel was born in 1791. He married Anna Marie Weiler, a woman later referred to as Louise.[5] Their third child, Albert Gottlieb Trostel, was born on November 26, 1834, in Unterberken, Wurttemberg.[6] According to the family tree, Albert Trostel was the only one of the Trostels' five children to leave Germany and find his fortune in America.[7]

Albert was one of many Germans who chose to leave their country in the mid-1800s, partially because of a long and unsuccessful social uprising that ended in 1849. Years before, following the defeat of Napoleon, European powers had divided Germany into 35 independent monarchies and four Free Cities. Border restrictions between these 39 small areas hindered transportation and communication, essentially holding inhabitants in an economic prison that prevented the kind of growth and development occurring elsewhere in the Western world. In rural communities, land was owned by the aristocracy and the church, relegating farmers like the Trostel family to a lifetime of servitude.[8]

In this world of quiet, moderately comfortable but uninspired living, with its strict social order and economic regulations, Georg and Anna Marie Trostel found the means and the motivation to move young Albert out of the family's agricultural traditions and into a trade. They provided him with an education and found him a tanning apprenticeship.[9]

Meanwhile, the Industrial Revolution inspired thoughtful, progressive men around the world to seek new freedoms and rights for ordinary citizens. Noting that voting males in England and the United States were already enjoying individual rights, German intellectuals formed a movement similar to their contemporaries in Poland and France who were demanding democratic institutions. While the German citizenry was initially disinterested in politics, these rebels pursued their cause, calling for elimination of the small monarchies and city-states in favor of German reunification. Arguing on behalf of their strong, cohesive cultural heritage and against the repression of German people, these persistent advocates of freedom encouraged students to join in the pursuit of people's rights. Citing the need for religious freedom, elimination of feudalism, open commerce, and a free press, students were heard around the country as they raised the cry for liberty and national unity.[10]

The movement gained momentum, goaded by the successful French Revolution of 1848.[11] That year, however, Prussian King Frederick William IV's army crushed the seeds of the radical revolt. Rebels retired to Stuttgart to continue their efforts but were soon disbanded by the military. Local militias, aided by the Prussian army, quashed other uprisings around the country.[12]

German Immigration to Milwaukee

After the failure of the 1848 rebellion, a number of defeated rebels, calling themselves "48ers," refused to return to German life under its repressive governments and took their know-how and strong ideals to America. In addition to the 48ers, struggling farmers and their families left their homeland for the New World. Albert Trostel was among the thousands of Germans who flooded the shores of America. In 1854, German immigration peaked at 252,000 people.[13]

Like earlier settlers, the immigrants wanted good homes for their families and stable communities with schools and churches. They were eager for the freedom and opportunity to build wealth and demonstrate the potential of their talent and the strength of their character.

The German immigrants filled Milwaukee with men and women of talent and vision. They founded German newspapers, such as the *Humanist*, the *Volkfreund*, the *Wiskonsin Banner*, and the *Seebot* to express the diverse views of the city's growing German population.[14]

Germans tended to settle in two areas of Milwaukee: the South Side and the Northwest Side. That left the east side for the Yankees and the third ward enclave for the Irish.[15] The Germans were proud of their heritage. Many who arrived were well-educated and believed it was their responsibility to bring culture and intellectualism to the less fortunate frontiersmen. In addition to German-language newspapers, books were published in German, and academic discourse flowed in the language of Schiller and Goethe. The new immigrants established churches, museum and singing societies, literary clubs, and German-language theaters. Musically, they favored German composers such as Beethoven, Mozart, and Mendelssohn.[16]

Their fierce loyalty to their mother country sometimes irritated the immigrants' new neighbors. For many years, these nationalistic Germans had very little interaction or intermarriage with their Yankee and Irish neighbors and boasted about the military victories "back in the homeland," sparking Yankees to charge that the Germans needed to learn English and blend with their new compatriots.[17]

In spite of their old-country nationalism, the Germans worked hard on behalf of their new city. They established a Catholic diocese in Milwaukee in 1844, and three years later raised the funds to build the landmark St. John's Cathedral, facing what was then Juneau's courthouse square. The Order of St. Francis seminary was established in 1855 to train German-speaking priests, and land was purchased on the west side for what would become Marquette University, which was chartered in 1864.[18]

Milwaukee's Industries

The Miller and Schlitz families—names familiar to contemporary beer drinkers—would soon enter the brewing business. In all, the beer industry brought more fame to Milwaukee than any other kind of production would.[19]

A drawing of Milwaukee in 1853, the year after Albert Trostel moved to the city. By this time, it held a robust population of recent German immigrants. *(Milwaukee County Historical Society)*

In terms of big profits and losses, though, wheat was king of the Milwaukee economy. Once the Wisconsin farmland began producing more wheat than the area could consume, and as soon as the harbor could accommodate large-scale commercial shipping, Milwaukee became a major wheat supplier to North America and the rest of the world.[20]

Wisconsin farmers also found livestock to be a profitable business. By the 1850s, cattle and hog butchering had become a major industry. Between 1840 and 1850, Wisconsin farmers increased their cattle production from 30,000 to more than 185,000. Similarly, the number of hogs raised rose from 51,000 to 160,000.[21]

That kind of production inspired individuals in the meat business to expand beyond retailing and warehousing into packing-house production. John Plankinton's small street-side meat market grew to become a vast slaughtering and packing business that in 1863 was the fourth-largest establishment of its kind in the country. Similarly, Frederick Layton, Michael Cudahy, and Philip Armour all began businesses in Milwaukee.[22] In 1871, Milwaukee was the number-four supplier of meat in the country.[23]

All of these industries would play a role in the Trostel family business. Wheat fed the cattle that provided the hides. The Schlitz brewery would eventually be taken over by the Uihlein family, whose descendent, Clara, would marry Albert Gottlieb Trostel's son, Albert O. Trostel, and prove to be a major force for the company well into the 20th century.

Tanning Industry

The natural outgrowth of the packing business, especially in an area rich with hemlock bark and with a generous water supply, was the tanning business. Leather was essential to life in the new country. In addition to its use in the construction of boots, shoes, and slippers, leather was used to bind books and to outfit men with breeches and ladies with gloves. Leather also provided saddles, bridles, a vast array of carriage parts, (including tops and seats), and ship riggings. Further, the process of leather production aided the farming and agricultural industries. Clearing forests to harvest tanning bark opened fields for cultivation. When tanners purchased hides from packing houses, they raised the value of livestock and improved profits for farmers.[24]

In addition to offering the raw materials necessary for leather production, Milwaukee boasted a plentiful labor supply. The immigrants who streamed into the area were eager to work and make a living. These men would toil at any job, no matter how backbreaking the task or undesirable the surroundings.

By 1850 Milwaukee was fast becoming a leader in America's tanning industry. Among the first leather merchants in the city were partners Rufus Allen and Edward P. Allis, Yankee tanners who arrived from New York state in the mid-1840s.[25] The census reported 8,229 tanneries in the country at the time, and some areas in the East were already running short of the bark used in the tanning process.[26] Eastern tanners, especially forward-

Pfister and Vogel Leather Company, Milwaukee's largest tannery, was headquartered in the Menomonee Valley. Trostel, on the other hand, located his operation closer to the Milwaukee River area, which would later become downtown. *(Milwaukee County Historical Society)*

thinking and adventurous individuals, sought to relocate near a better supply of resources.[27] The tanning methods the Yankees brought to Milwaukee were thought by some to be primitive compared to those of their European contemporaries. Smithsonian Institution records cite early New England documents depicting local tanneries as somewhat disorganized, their vats roughly made, and their tools crude.[28]

When Germans like Trostel arrived, however, the tanning process evolved into a sophisticated industry. Immigrating German tanners had apprenticed with Old World craftsmen in a country of high workmanship standards. Together, they formed the backbone of the remarkable tanning industry that developed in Milwaukee. Frederick Vogel and Guido Pfister were the first notable tanning entrepreneurs in the thriving Wisconsin city. Both men came from Wurttemberg, Germany, the birthplace of Albert Gottlieb Trostel.[29]

Like many other German immigrants, Pfister and Vogel were well-connected financially and came to Milwaukee with investor backing. The men began their work in the Buffalo, New York, tannery of Vogel's cousin, J. F. Schoellkopf, a supporter of the young men's Milwaukee venture. Pfister came to Milwaukee with $500 to start his business. On March 24, 1848, he wrote to an unidentified relative in Germany.

We will form a company consisting of Schoellkopf, his cousin Vogel and myself and will operate a large tannery at this place, for which I have already bought two acres of land for $700. Vogel will be the tanner and I will run a store and warehouse in the city to furnish the money and hides. Schoellkopf, who remains in Buffalo, will put in the $13,000 and supply us with everything we require from the east.

This is my condition as it shaped itself in the short time during my stay in this rich, peaceable country, and if we meet good success in the tannery it will improve from day to day.

To express myself briefly, everybody in this country who is active, honest and attends to his business will find assistance, in contrast to Germany where only those who can hold their heads high in the air will be helped along.[30]

In 1847, while Pfister set up shop, Vogel started tanning cow hides—not buffalo skins—in a tannery in the Menomonee Valley. Sources differ on the timing of their association, but they most likely purchased interest in each other's operations in the late 1850s and merged as Pfister and Vogel sometime in the early 1860s.[31] The resulting company would become a longtime leader in world leather production.

In contrast to his competition, Albert Gottlieb Trostel arrived in Milwaukee at age 18 with barely a penny in his pocket. Yet he came as a well-trained and skilled craftsman with an education. Initially he farmed to support himself, while also working at the William Schroeder tannery. After four years of hard work, he had saved enough money to lease the operation from Schroeder and set about creating a business of his own.[32]

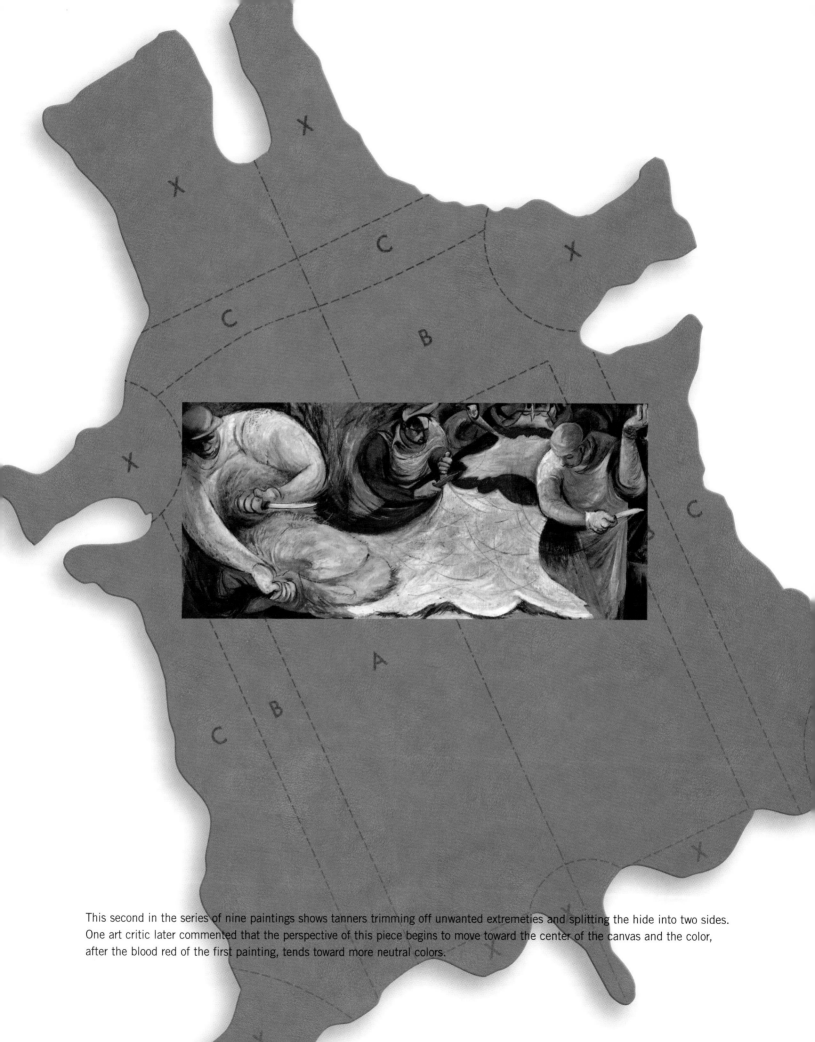

This second in the series of nine paintings shows tanners trimming off unwanted extremeties and splitting the hide into two sides. One art critic later commented that the perspective of this piece begins to move toward the center of the canvas and the color, after the blood red of the first painting, tends toward more neutral colors.

CHAPTER TWO

THE TANNERY

1860 – 1900

In Milwaukee, there is no more respected citizen than Albert Trostel, and the business that he has built up is known all over the country.

—The Successful American

A YEAR AFTER SAVING enough money to lease a tannery and venture into business on his own, Albert Trostel formed a partnership with his friend August Gallun. The association, which began in 1858, was to last 27 years.[1]

Their partnership couldn't have come at a better time, as leather was proving to be quite the growth industry in Milwaukee. In 1859, Milwaukee had nine tanneries, and leather production totaled $217,500 in value. A year later, leather production ranked among Milwaukee's most important industries, behind flour and meal.[2] By 1872, the city was producing more leather than any other city in the world.[3]

Trostel and Gallun began with the production of saddle leather in a small 20-by-20-foot space at the end of Milwaukee's Jefferson Street. Over the next three years, the two men became well-known for their production of "Blue Star" leather, used for saddles, reins, harnesses, and carriage fittings that were revered around the country for their high quality.[4]

Soon after Trostel and Gallun's partnership began, the Civil War broke out. Milwaukee was home base for 6,000 soldiers, creating an enormous local demand for supplies. Leather was needed for boots and everything necessary for horse-drawn transportation.[5] Fortunately, Trostel and the other Milwaukee tanners were well-prepared to supply all that leather,[6] and the industry benefited enormously from the tremendous influx of funds during the war years. The added capital was used to fund industrial improvements in tanning technology, mechanization, and plant expansion.[7]

In 1861, with demand for their leather so high, Trostel and Gallun moved to a location on North Water Street at the north end of Pere Marquette Park.[8] The new facility was called the Star Tannery. In 1865, the company suffered a large loss when the tannery was partially destroyed by fire. Newspaper reports say the fire began on April 5 in a neighboring icehouse. Before the fire could be contained and despite efforts of firefighters, who arrived immediately, high winds that day swept the flames into the tannery. Trostel and Gallun had purchased a good deal of new machinery for the factory, so losses were high. The newspaper said the owners expected to lose more than the $15,000 for which the operation was insured. That same

The earliest Albert Trostel tannery. This one, like the next two, was claimed by a fire, forcing the partners to rebuild.

year, the Star Tannery was rebuilt on a much larger scale.[9]

The Rise of Milwaukee

As the Civil War drew to a close in 1865 and the country stabilized somewhat, Milwaukee was progressing as one of the key commercial cities in the Midwest. By the late 1860s, an Ohio journalist noted Milwaukee's significance as an urban center.

One of the wonders of the 19th century is the growth of American cities. Twenty-eight years ago, Milwaukee was a small, unimportant village, situated on two bluffs and divided by a sluggish river and an almost impenetrable tamarack swamp. Now, on the same ground, stands the home of a hundred thousand busy people; and in the midst of the tamarack swamp the most luxurious hotel west of New York. On the very spot where thirty years ago the Indians exchanged their furs for trinkets is being built a block of offices at an outlay of over a quarter of a million. In view of what has been done, and with our augmented facilities, what may we not expect in the coming thirty years?[10]

As intent as the citizens of Milwaukee were on building a prosperous community, they remained relatively remote and mostly provincial and individualistic. In the mid-1870s, decades before the advent of the automobile, New York was nearly 48 hours away. The resolute sailed to Chicago, rode the Michigan Southern railroad to Toledo, took a steamer to Buffalo, and then proceeded to New York aboard an "express train." That trek doubtless impeded the Eastern metropolises from influencing much of Milwaukee's development.[11]

Milwaukee celebrated its 30th birthday in 1876. The "workingman's city," as Milwaukee was now known, boasted high wages and encouraged families to own their own homes. Germans rightly believed that business ownership was not a prerequisite for financial achievement. Once a man had acquired a trade, they said, he was his own kind of capitalist. Plumbers, for example, could earn $4 a day, and carpenters $3 a day. Shop workers such as cabinetmakers worked 10- to 12-hour days for $2.25. Tannery and brewery workers were well-paid, too, with tannery straw bosses earning as much as $18

A view of Milwaukee Bay around the turn of the century. Between the 1850s and the early 20th century, Milwaukee grew rapidly yet retained a uniquely Teutonic flavor. *(Milwaukee County Historical Society)*

The Trostel and Gallun tannery. From here, the partners produced "Blue Star" leather, which was used in saddles, harnesses, carriage fittings, and various other products. *(Milwaukee Journal-Sentinel)*

for a six-day week, and brewery workers between $40 and $50 a month. A brewery foreman could earn as much as $3,000 a year and enjoy a benefit extended to all brewery workers—all the beer they could drink on the job.[12]

Hard work took its toll, however. In 1886, 14,000 Milwaukee workers went on strike, demanding an eight-hour day. Fearing the strike might lead to a riot, authorities closed the saloons, something that rarely happened in Milwaukee, and the state militia was called out to enforce order. When shots were fired into the crowd, four men and a child were killed. The workers felt the shooting was unprovoked and excessive, but the governor exclaimed that he would do what was necessary to protect property and ensure that all citizens obeyed the laws of the state.[13]

Throughout the strife and negotiation, Milwaukee industry thrived. Many Germans, plus a few Yankees were responsible for propelling Milwaukee into a leadership position in the leather industry. Rufus Allen from Massachusetts founded the Wisconsin Leather Company, at one time the largest producer of harness leather in the country. Other than Allen, however, it was the Germans—Albert Gottlieb Trostel and August F. Gallun, Guido Pfister and Fred Vogel, Roman Sulm, and Herman Zohrlaut—who were the esteemed leaders of the tanning business.[14]

A horse-drawn fire wagon. In the early days of Trostel's
business, fire was an ever-present hazard. Trostel's first two
tanneries were destroyed or severely damaged by fire.
(Milwaukee County Historical Society)

Another Fire

Trostel and Gallun celebrated Milwaukee's 30th
anniversary with a key purchase—a property known
as the Old Paper Mill at 893 to 903 Water Street.
They remodeled and converted the building into the
Empire Tannery. But fires were common in those
days, and on New Year's Day 1881, the Trostel and
Gallun partnership suffered an even bigger loss
when the converted paper mill burned.

The *Milwaukee Sentinel* reported that the fire
started at 9:30 A.M. An engineer and one employee
who were in the building were the first to observe
the fire. According to the newspaper reports, the
employee had left a lamp burning over the boilers
near an outside wall. The fire began burning that
wall and swiftly moved through the wooden venti-
lating flues to engulf the building in flames. The
roof was ablaze before firemen arrived, a situation
attributed to the fact that the two workers at first
believed they could manage the flames with chemical extinguishers.[15]

Losses were estimated at $3,500 for the build-
ing plus $18,000 of the $50,000 worth of stock.
The entire operation was insured for $30,100, but
only $17,000 of that was for stock. "Mssrs. Trostel
and Gallun claim that they suffered a much heav-
ier loss than the superficial observer would believe,"
the newspaper reported. "Their pits were all filled
with stock in process of manufacture and these
pits or vats were all flooded."[16]

Overcoming the disaster, the partners purchased Milwaukee Hide and Leather Company on

Commerce Street in 1882. That building had also been partially burned, so they rebuilt it. After enlargement and refitting, the operation was renamed the Phoenix Tannery.[17] There the company produced boot leather.[18]

Leather's Progress: 1880s and 1890s

Trostel and Gallun's continued ability to rebuild and expand their facilities in the wake of disaster could be attributed to the growth of their operation, as well as that of Milwaukee's entire tanning industry, which made significant strides during the last two decades of the 19th century, a period known as the "decade of manufacturing advance" in Milwaukee[19] and a time of exceptional prosperity.[20] In addition to the earnings the industry brought to owners and employers, it spawned other manufac-

turing, all contributing greatly to the financial growth and development of the city.[21] For example, the tanneries supplied leather for the local shoe firm of Bradley and Metcalf. Started by two Yankees in 1843, the sprawling factory had become one of the largest shoe and boot manufacturers in the Northwest. The largest tannery orders, however, came from the gigantic New England shoe factories.

By 1890 the huge demand made Milwaukee the largest producer of plain tanned leather in the world.[22] Milwaukee's output totaled $8.43 million. Chicago was in second place with a production totaling $7.3 million. Allegany, Pennsylvania, was third, followed by Louisville, San Francisco, Newark, and Buffalo.[23]

With the industry growing, local tanneries could not afford to maintain the status quo. They were bound to either expand and improve or fall by the wayside. Consequently, many small tanneries, without the means or motivation to become big businesses, had closed their doors by 1890, opening opportunities for progressive factories like Trostel's. This movement in favor of bigger operations reduced the number of tanneries in

---

The Phoenix Tannery, which later became the company's main plant, remained with Trostel after he and Gallun parted ways. The tannery was located on Commerce Street.

the city from 30 in 1872 to 15 in 1886. Milwaukee's output swelled from 102,570 hides in 1865 to 533,357 in 1886.[24] The Trostel tannery played a major role in this 500 percent increase.

The growth and development process was not without bumps. The panic of 1893 was especially severe in Milwaukee. Five banks had to close their doors; three never reopened.[25] No manufacturing companies failed, but many cut wages.[26] The tanning companies were hit hard, but business began showing improvement in 1895 and had recovered completely two years later.[27]

By 1897, production of hides reached the 1 million mark per year. Milwaukee tanneries were unstoppable in their quest for increased profits and industrial power. Wisconsin farmers were unable to supply enough hides. As orders for leather skyrock-eted, packing houses from Chicago, Kansas City, Omaha, and even Europe sent railway carloads and boatloads of hides to Milwaukee,[28] whose tanneries were refitted for improved efficiency. After 1890, the owners created larger production units and installed machinery. They also shortened the tanning process; previously, heavy hides had taken three years to process, but they were now completed in eight months. Tanners began importing tannin extract by rail and ship, using it extensively in place of the ever-diminishing supply of tanbark.[29]

Milwaukee: 1880s and 1890s

Of course, Milwaukee's tanning industry could not have grown during the late 19th century if the city itself hadn't grown. By 1880, it was

MAKING LEATHER

HUMANKIND WAS MAKING LEATHER long before history was recorded. The earth's earliest human inhabitants produced leather shoes, clothes, tents, beds, rugs, and bags to keep people and their possessions fresh and cool.[1] Leather production continued and was refined throughout the centuries. By the time the Greeks were tanning leather, their processes were being recorded, giving today's leather-makers insight into the millennia-old craft.

Greek tanning, in fact, was not so different from methods that are currently used. New hides were packed flat with powdered ground bark between the layers, sometimes with the addition of roots and berries. These "pickling" hides were left for months before they were unpacked, hung on poles, and then smoothed with rolling pins. The Greek tanneries were located outside the city walls so that wet skins could be spread on the ground where people walked to and from the city. These ingenious leather roadways resulted in softened leather. Finished skins were shipped off to the leather cutters who were considered among the finest artisans in the country. The great libraries of Rome and Constantinople exhibit stunning examples of their works, including handsome books bound in tooled leather covers that were encrusted with jewels.[2]

Following the Greek tradition of assigning status to leather makers, early Christians elevated one such craftsman to their highest honor. Saint Crispin, who was descended from a noble Roman family, was a shoemaker in Soissons, France, where he spread the Christian word through acts of charity, allegedly stealing leather to make shoes for the poor.[3]

Because of its practical applications, leather making became a highly developed craft among indigenous people around the globe. When the Europeans discovered the New World, Native Americans were already accomplished leather-makers. For the most part, the work was done by women who collected the hides, stacked them in piles, wet them, and allowed them to decompose until the hair was loosened. Then the hides were scraped with bone tools until the flesh and hair were removed. The softening was accomplished clear that Milwaukee had experienced a remarkable population boom. One hundred thousand people lived in the city, many of whom fueled the leather industry, by either providing labor or purchasing products.

The city's growth and the mix of German- and American-born citizens—more than half were native-born—could have been volatile, but a growing tolerance for other nationalities was detectable. In forging relationships across old-country lines, Milwaukeeans softened the boundaries between wards and eased old tensions. They began to unify as they found themselves taking pride in their new city.[30]

However, while some Germans added English phrases to their native language and the German community was no longer completely tied to the old country, the Germans were not about to be bullied into their new citizenry.

This new generation, emboldened by Germany's victory in the Franco-Prussian War, was more confident than its 48er forebears. Its wealth was imposing and its voting blocks determined election outcomes.[31] When state legislation in 1890 required students to attend neighborhood schools and be instructed in English, German voters ousted all the legislators that had voted for the measure and had their new representatives repeal the law.

The Milwaukee of 1890—and, indeed, well into the 20th century—benefited from the good nature and fortitude of its German population and retained the Teutonic flavor of its origins. U.S. census reports published in 1890 claim that Milwaukee, with a population of 204,468, was the

---

by rubbing a mixture of animal brains and livers on the hides until they were thoroughly supple. The Crow Indians, considered to be America's most advanced tanners, immersed the hides in a lye solution as the final step, then stacked them in a tightly closed teepee for smoking, which was the final cure.[4]

The Industrial Revolution, of course, transformed the localized craft into a huge industry. Massive factories with mechanized production were built to produce leather in vast quantities. It was not until the 1800s, though, that innovators discovered the process that would propel leather from a practical to a luxury item. This innovation came at the hands of two Americans. Chemist August Schultz found that if chromium rather than white alum were used to tan leather it would retain its color when wet, thus shortening the tanning process considerably. Perfecting that process, Philadelphia tanner Robert Foerderer used soap and oil to make chromium-tanned leather soft and supple.[5]

Leather tanned by means of these new industrial methods was perfectly suited to the luxury markets. No marvel of science had yet to produce leather's equal, a paradoxical product that was porous while it was absorptive, and tough while it was supple and beautiful.

This remarkable product of nature began its upscale movement in the 1950s. On April 20, 1955, the *Milwaukee Journal* ran a feature spread on the fashionable leather produced at Albert Trostel & Sons' Milwaukee tannery. The full-page article, "Romance in Leather," was, like the leather products about to hit the markets, uncharacteristically colorful. "Some very unglamorous beginnings result in what is glamour to most women," *Journal* staffer Lucille Preuss wrote. The article, which was spread across the front page of the fashion and society section, displayed photos of men and women in the tannery producing the vibrantly colored leather.[6]

Preuss eloquently proposed one reason leather was moving up in status. "The language of leather is one a woman can understand," she wrote. The newspaper detailed the Trostel process. Preuss reported how cured

 hides arrived at the tannery preserved in salt and then headed for their first grading, this time according to weight. Following that, they were cut in half down the backbone. The resulting pieces, called sides, were sorted into loads of about 2,250 pounds each.[7]

nation's most foreign city at the time.[32] On October 6, 1890, 12,000 Germans marched in the city's German Day parade, the largest turnout ever.[33] And it wasn't just the German population displaying civic pride. In 1891, *Cosmopolitan* noted, "There is not of its size in all America a city that contains a population more self-respecting, more law-abiding, more cheerful and content than Milwaukee."[34]

Milwaukeeans also enjoyed the product of their breweries. One of the most popular places for entertainment in the 1890s was the Schlitz Palm Garden. An immense and spectacular indoor facility, the garden featured a high domed ceiling with elaborate light fixtures, windows of stained glass, and life-size potted palm trees. The furnishings included ornate oil paintings and a multitude of white-covered tables, where Sunday patrons delighted in food, drink, and live musical entertainment.[35]

Milwaukee in 1890 was known as the "Cream City of the Lakes," from the yellowish hue of the bricks used to construct many of its buildings. In contrast to the brown and red masonry of other metropolitan areas, writers noted, Milwaukee's sunny-colored buildings gave it a particularly light and cheerful appearance. The simplicity of those yellow structures gave the city an overall architectural flavor of propriety rather than flamboyance.[36] "Steady-going plodders, with their love for music and flowers, [German Milwaukeeans] have yet no keen taste for display, and every time choose the substantial rather than the ornamental," wrote Willard Glazier in *Peculiarities of American Cities*.[37]

Leather processing proceeded, using as much mechanization as possible. The loads of hides were then dumped through an iron grate and into large drums for soaking. After between two and 48 hours,[8] the hides were cleansed of salt, softened, and treated to prevent bacterial contamination. Following the drum bath, the hides were taken to the "beam house." This term dated to the earliest days of tanning and referred to the place where the hair was removed. Here, following century-old tanning traditions, loose flesh was scraped from the hides before they were soaked in vats. The soaking took place for 12 to 48 hours, depending on the weight of the hides.[9]

The hard work continued in the beam house. The vat processing loosened the hair and more of  the flesh before the workers again scraped the hides with special knives. The scraped hair was said to look like the old rug pads that indeed were a byproduct of the process.[10]

The "bate, pickle, and tan" departments were next. These steps were considered to be the actual tanning, the places where the hide became leather. First, the bate neutralized the hides, stopping the chemical action of the hair-

and flesh-removal  process. In vats filled with warm water and bating material, hides were turned with paddles for as long as four hours before becoming completely neutralized,[11] after which they were piled flat and allowed to drain.[12]

Following the bating, the hides moved into the final two phases of actual tanning.[13] The first of those steps was the pickle process that opened the pores of the hides, preparing them to receive the tanning ingredients. For pickling, hides were soaked in a solution of acid and common salt for four to eight hours, again with paddle wheels in the vats turning the hides throughout. Pickling further neutralized the lime and also drew the moisture out of the hides. Finally, chromium was used for tanning. With that tanning ingredient, hides emerged a blue color.[14]

After tanning, the leather was once again sorted, this time according to end use. The sides were split by machine. The top pieces had the fine grain and were used for ladies' leather clothing and accessories. The lower pieces were used for work gloves and shoes, and also for less expensive suede items. The split leather was sorted by

Trostel and Gallun: Marriage and Family

Albert Trostel and August Gallun played their part in the population boom. They, too, married and had families, thereby establishing permanent roots in Milwaukee. August F. Gallun was born in Germany on May 30, 1834, into a long line of tanners. After the failed revolution in their native country, several members of the Gallun family were inspired to leave home and sail for America. August Gallun worked for a time in Yonkers, New York, before heading to the Midwest. After a brief stay in Chicago, he came to Milwaukee, where he completed his education and became partners with Albert Trostel.[38]

Gallun was active in the community. He was listed as a member of the city board of supervisors in 1875.[39] Reportedly, he appreciated the liberty and opportunity presented to him in his new country and showed his gratitude by helping immigrant workers assimilate. While the practice was not always popular among his peers, he persisted. He was said to have worked hard to help his employees purchase homes in Milwaukee.[40]

In 1864, Gallun married Julia Kraus, a young woman who came to America with her parents in 1849. They had four children—Albert F., Ella, Edwin A., and Arthur H. Edwin—who died in an accident at the age of 22.

Albert Trostel was also very supportive of the local community. Newspapers identified him as a Republican and listed memberships in the Deutsche Gesellschaft, the Old Settlers' Club, the German and English Academy Association, and the United

thickness and then colored accordingly. Base coats varied from shades of brown or beige to white, depending on the intensity and shade of the hue that would follow. And once again, the moisture was squeezed from the leather.[15]

With the leather separated according to use, the hides were ready for drying. At this point, the Native Americans would peg hides to the ground. At the Trostel tannery, hides were sprayed with a white paste consisting of flour, water,  and other ingredients. Using a dull metal squeegee, the hides were then smoothed onto large glass plates before being forced through heated tunnels for drying. Coming out of the drying tunnels, the leather was stiff and dry, so once again it needed to be moisturized. Washing machines were used for the two-fold process of paste-removal and leather-hydration.[16]

Once hydrated, some of the hides were sent to be staked, a process reserved for hides that needed to be soft and flexible. Work-shoe leather, for example, was never staked. The process of staking essentially rearranged the fibers in the leather, something Eskimos were known to accomplish by chewing the hides. In the tannery, wooden paddles rolled and pulled the hides until the level of desired suppleness was attained.

After staking, the soft leather was sanded. Inside a roller, sandpaper evened out the leather, smoothed out the rough spots, and opened the pores, preparing the skins for further treatment. All leather, except for that which was full grained, was treated here before it proceeded into the world of hues.[17]

After coloring, the leather was sent for plating. The plating machine applied heat and pressure in one of the last steps. A piece could be plated as many as three times. The step gave the leather its luster and permanency. Finally the leather was finished with a top spray, then a dressing and finally waterproofing. At the end of the factory line, the leather was sorted for the last time, graded, and shipped out. The brilliantly colored pieces were made into the shoes, handbags, and belts that were becoming the rage in the fashion world.[18]

Workmen.[41] In 1863, Albert Trostel married A. F. Gallun's sister, Charlotte. Born September 4, 1832, in Osterwiek, Germany, she later immigrated to America. Charlotte and Albert had four children—Gustav, Albert O., Ida, and Otto, who died in infancy in 1871.[42]

According to stories written on one family tree and mentioned in some publications, the children of the two partners did not get along. Reportedly, the main conflict existed between Albert F. Gallun, who was born in 1865, and Albert O. Trostel, who was born in 1866. Other reports tell of hard feelings between A. F. Gallun's wife and Ida, the daughter of Albert and Charlotte Trostel. Apparently, the women were so angry with each other that they never attended the same party.[43]

A Split

By all accounts, Albert G. Trostel and A. F. Gallun had an amiable relationship and remained friends all their lives. However, due to the disagreements among their family members, Trostel and Gallun ended their partnership on May 1, 1885, with Gallun taking the company office and the Empire Tannery. There he specialized in fine calf leathers and built a successful business for his family. Trostel retained the Star Tannery, on North Water Street, as well as the Phoenix Tannery, on the canal.[44] *Industrial History of Milwaukee,* 1886, says of the property that went to Trostel:

The main buildings are respectively 60 feet by 150 feet and 60 feet by 300 feet, besides the necessary buildings, land and dockage to accommodate his supplies, and his immense stock of bark, the majority of which he receives by vessel from Michigan while the lake is open to navigation.[45]

The article elaborated on the expansiveness of Trostel's two factories. According to the report, the Trostel operations were fitted with all the modern leather-producing equipment of the period. Each

tannery contained a 40-horsepower engine and four large boilers to drive the machinery. At the time, the business employed between 150 and 200 men. The operation "turn[s] out annually upwards of 65,000 sides, kips, and calf skins, all of the best green, and green salted Western slaughter stock, which calls for the use of 8,000 cords of bark."[46]

The *Industrial History* article goes on to describe the products of the tannery, which included "russet and black harness, saddle, collar and line leather, boot and shoe grains, wax upper, kip and calf skins."[47]

In fact, the shape of Trostel's future was being forged: no frills for this tannery. Rather, Trostel's would emphasize those leathers which "did" things, working leather so to speak: leather which supported hauling by horse, by carriage, mechanical leather to be used in automobiles, sturdy leather for boots to be worn by marching soldiers.[48]

Because Gallun got the company store when the partners separated, Trostel was in need of a retail location to sell his products. Besides the production of leather, the company at that time was retailing "findings, tanners' and curriers' tools and supplies, oils, etc."[49] Consequently, Trostel purchased a four-story brick building at 104 West Water Street, then a location near the Huron Street Bridge. Trostel outfitted the store in excellent taste, according to the *Industrial History* article, and put together an attractive and functional establishment. Sales were promising, and the store attracted a national clientele. The company had annual sales at the time of approximately $500,000, and carried stock with the value of $200,000 to $300,000.[50]

A. F. Gallun was partners with Albert Trostel for nearly three decades, beginning in 1858. He remained close friends with Trostel even after their partnership was dissolved.
(Milwaukee County Historical Society)

In 1892, the two Trostel tanneries were producing a large variety of leather products, as listed in *Milwaukee's Great Industries.*

In these tanneries are produced fine grain leathers; wax leathers; hemlock harness leather; black and russet collar and casing leather; grain and flesh-finished fly-net; russet and colored skirting; bridle, line and strap in oiled or fair stock; fair russet pad leather; russet legging; and saddle bag, scabbard and lace leather.[51]

At this point, tanning's contribution to the Milwaukee economy was considerable. According to Henry Eskuche's 1892 account, "Leather and the Tanning Industry," 3,000 men produced $7 million worth of leather. Woodchoppers and other laborers felled 350,000 hemlock trees annually to supply tanning bark. Shipping the raw materials and finished product fueled yet another industry.[52]

Trostel continued expanding, eventually tripling the size and capacity of his plants. In 1895, the company procured a canal tannery owned by Pfister and Vogel. The partnership of Pfister and Vogel, who had merged their tanning and retail businesses in 1847, was a very large and lucrative organization that dwarfed Trostel's plant.[53] However, the majority of their large operation was clustered in the Menomonee Valley, some distance to the south and west of the Trostel tanneries. The sale of the canal property, so important to Trostel, probably enhanced the business of both tanneries. The new purchase, eventually called the Commerce Street factory, commenced production May 1, 1896, and became the center of the firm's operations. With the additional factory, Trostel's growing company was expected to have a workforce of 600 men.[54]

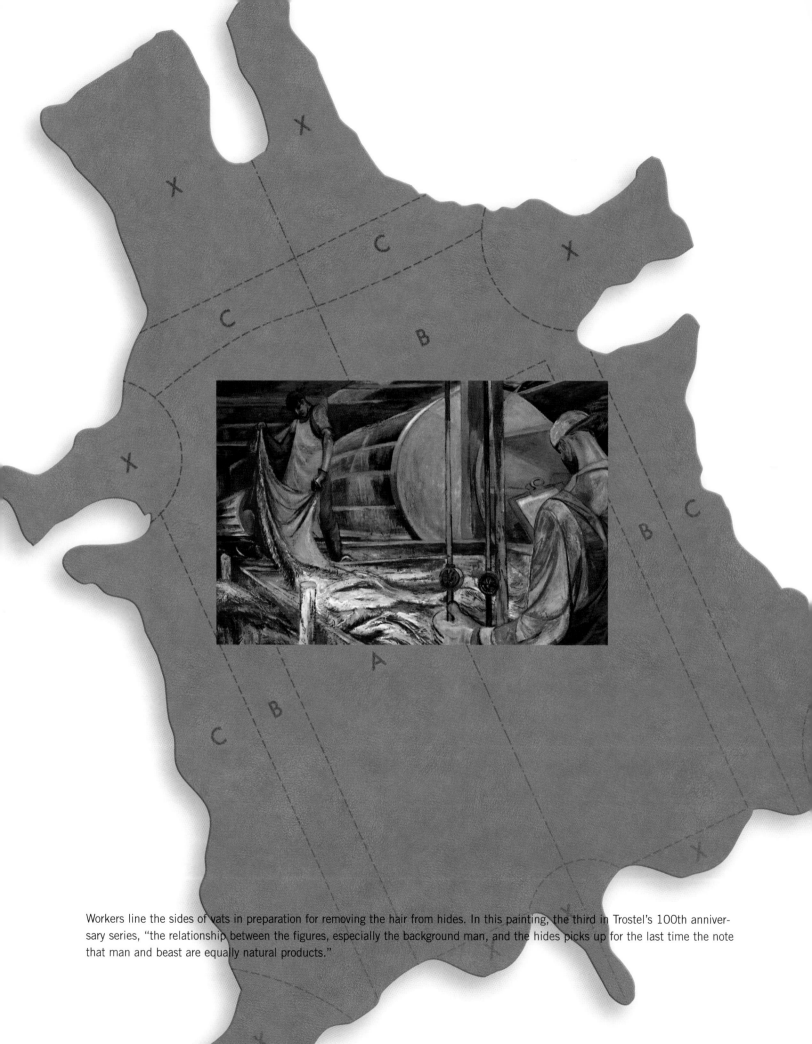

Workers line the sides of vats in preparation for removing the hair from hides. In this painting, the third in Trostel's 100th anniversary series, "the relationship between the figures, especially the background man, and the hides picks up for the last time the note that man and beast are equally natural products."

CHAPTER THREE

CHANGING OF THE GUARD

1900 – 1919

*No Manufacturer of Medium or Fine Grade Shoes or Harness can
afford not to become fully acquainted with our Leathers. They Always
Please Everyone, because they represent the Highest Attainments of
Tanning Experience.*

—Early 20th-century Trostel advertisement

MILWAUKEEANS WERE PROUD of the array and wide use of their city's leathers. In more than 15 leather-industry trade journals, Milwaukee was prominently listed as the maker of harnesses, collars, and leggings. Additionally, Milwaukee was a featured producer of leather for saddle skirting and line and fly-net leather. Cowboys working on the Plains as far west as New Mexico and as far south as Texas used Milwaukee leather. In addition, the large horse-collar factories of Chicago, St. Louis, and St. Paul were dependent on Milwaukee leather for production of fittings. "The farmer's horse, the Southern mule, the fine Percheron teams of the brewers, as well as stylish coach horses, are decked with harness, collars and fly-nets made out of the always-reliable Milwaukee leather."[1]

As a major player in Milwaukee's tanning industry, Trostel had access to the finest hides available. Midwestern hides were thought to be far superior to those produced in the South because the conditions in which cattle were raised and fed produced a better textured and firmer hide.[2]

The Successful American, in a 1901 printing, gave a flowery yet hard-driving tribute to the success of Albert Trostel and his peers.

The subject ... is one of that sturdy type of German-Americans who, by their industry, perse-

verance and thrift, have amassed fortunes and established for their families lucrative businesses. Their example is a fitting one to the ambitious youth, and their success demonstrates what any honest, persevering young man with all the benefits of a modern education can do with proper application; for have they not every advantage over the men who came here unfamiliar with our language and customs? In Milwaukee, there is no more respected citizen than Albert Trostel, and the business that he has built up is known all over the country.[3]

The residential neighborhoods, with their tasteful but unpretentious homes, were lined with trees, which added a stately, friendly beauty.[4] Further, the city decided in 1896 to pave all streets with granite, brick, or asphalt, yet another enhancement to the pretty neighborhoods.[5] Home ownership was an important factor in the city's stability. In the 1890s, almost all families owned homes, no matter how small, making Milwaukee a national leader in home ownership.[6] The city reported 40,000 homes for its 260,000 people in 1890.[7]

Gustav Trostel, son of Albert Trostel and president of the Trostel tannery, built this house on Terrace Avenue and Belleview Place. The house featured a ballroom and spectacular lake views.

Albert and Charlotte Trostel

One of Milwaukee's tonier homes belonged to the Trostel family. In 1863, Albert and Charlotte Trostel, the sister of A. F. Gallun,[8] lived at 1648 North Jackson Street in an Italianate house still standing in 2004. In 1903, some additions were made in the Colonial Revival style.[9] The home stands on a hill that, at the time, was located a few blocks from Trostel's tannery buildings. One can imagine the proud industrialist walking to and from his tanneries each day.

Gustav, Charlotte and Albert's eldest, was schooled in the German tradition and positioned to inherit leadership of the family business. According to company archives, he may have been sent to Germany as a teen for two years for the kind of tanning apprenticeship his father had completed decades earlier. Gustav never talked about this part of his life, but after his death, the Gallun family discovered photos in Frieburg, Germany, attesting that Gustav did apprentice there. It is known that Gustav's father's entire family of origin had remained in Germany, except for one brother.[10] All reports suggest that Albert very seriously set about training his sons in all aspects of the business and then proudly proclaimed them fully capable of continuing the company's success.[11]

Newspaper articles indicate that Albert O., born in 1866, was educated at the Peter Engelmann German-English School. Engelmann was a German revolutionary who edited a newspaper in his native land before immigrating to the United States. In Milwaukee, he turned to teaching, first in his home and then in a school built especially for his pupils.[12] The Engelmann School eventually became the University School of Milwaukee.[13]

After his children had reached adulthood, Albert Gottlieb Trostel suffered a tremendous loss when Charlotte died on February 7, 1899. She was described as the love of Albert's life and a woman of "noble and gentle character" who was adored by her family.[14] Remarkably, Albert remained active in the business almost until his own death on November 3, 1907.[15]

It was consistent with his character that he refused to retire when he approached the age of

70, but continued actively in the management of the business until his final illness brought his useful life to a close. He was one of the world's productive workers, large of heart and large of mind, and his memory will long be revered in the city in which he lived and labored for half a century.[16]

The senior Trostel was conservative in matters of character, his integrity never questioned. Albert strove throughout his life to increase the efficiency and productivity of the family business.[17]

Fortunately, before he passed away, Albert Trostel had brought his sons into the business. The Star Tannery on North Water had been expanded and now produced between 2,000 and 2,500 sides a week, providing leather mostly for horse-drawn transportation. The Phoenix Tannery, located across the river on Commerce Street, had a capacity of 4,500 sides, soon to increase to 6,000. That leather was destined for boots and shoes.[18] The company had weathered the national financial crisis known as the Panic of 1893 and moved into the new century with a flourish.

A New Century

By 1901, Milwaukee was booming. Its population had soared 400 percent during the preceding 40 years, and manufacturing production had topped $123 million.[19] The Albert Trostel & Sons Tannery was considered one of the largest plants in the country. Situated on 10 acres of ground,[20] the operations were housed in a four-story brick building of 500,000 square feet.[21] To promote its product, the company took out a half-page advertisement in an oversize book on Milwaukee business.

The World Wide Sale and High Reputation of Trostel's "STAR" and "PHOENIX" Leathers, proves their Exceptional Worth. We are continually placing upon the market new tannages of superlative beauty, superb finish and rare merit, and are always ready to submit samples of and quote prices on all of these superior leathers. No Manufacturer of Medium or Fine Grade Shoes or Harness can afford not to become fully acquainted with our Leathers. They Always Please Everyone, because they represent the Highest Attainments of Tanning Experience.[22]

This ad for Albert Trostel announces some of the company's well-known products, including the Blue Star brand. At the time, Trostel was a more retail oriented tannery than in later years. *(Milwaukee Public Library)*

During the first decade of the 20th century, Milwaukee presented great opportunity to Trostel and its competitors. There were more ships entering Milwaukee's ports than any other Great Lakes city except Chicago.[23] With the expansion of railroad networks, more markets ordered from Milwaukee.[24] This enabled Trostel and the other tanneries to respond to the national demand for their product, but they did a brisk local business as well, as evidenced by Milwaukee's growing shoe industry. In 1909, the F. Mayer Boot and Shoe Company had the capacity to produce 9,000 pairs of boots a day. In addition, Weyenberg Shoe Manufacturing Company produced heavy-duty workmen's boots, and Bradley and Metcalf produced upscale men's shoes that they sold for $4 a pair.[25]

At this time, many tanneries tried to consolidate their operations at one location; all adopted innovative methods of tanning and looked to manage their employees better. True to their hardworking, old-country roots, the German owners were diligent in their efforts to make their operations more profitable, while keeping quality high. Milwaukee's tannery production was valued at nearly $27.5 million.[26]

Second-Generation Trostels

By the time Albert Trostel died and his children were making their mark in society, Milwaukee's transformation from New World stand-in for Germany to Midwestern jewel was complete. The *Book of Milwaukee*, published in 1901, claimed that Milwaukee was no longer considered the "Cream

City of the Lakes." Rather it had become known as "Milwaukee the Beautiful." "Needless to say, it is no misnomer," continued the article. "Milwaukee is at once the most attractive, cleanest, freshest looking, and one might even say, the daintiest of American Cities. It is indeed the incomparable white city of the unsalted seas."[27]

Sons and daughters of the immigrants had shed many of the last vestiges of their parents old-country ways. Their education and emerging tastes, so different from those of their forebears, were becoming the accepted customs and traditions and were decidedly American. By the turn of the century, many younger Germans were native-born and English-speaking. They saw the value of a country with a common language and became increasingly critical of their ancestors who held so tightly to their native tongue.[28]

"Though the habits and traits of character still cling to them in some degree, their original nationality is soon lost."[29] A large part of the young generation's American identity was demonstrated in their homes. The location of the houses, the size of the construction, the character of the design, the quality of the materials, the workmanship in the finishing, and the luxury of the furnishings became an important indicator of prominence in the community.

The Trostel children, building on the wealthy company left to them by their father, were part of that up-and-coming generation of young Milwaukeeans. Albert and Charlotte's daughter, Ida, who was born in 1868, married Adolph Finkler. The couple had two children, Charlotte and Albert Trostel Finkler.[30] In 1918, Ida and Adolph bought Judge Paul Dillingham Carpenter's house at 2429 East Wyoming Place. The home was a large, stately English Tudor designed by Alexander C. Eschweiler and built in 1903 by Paul D. Carpenter, the son of a distinguished U.S. senator.

Adolph Finkler was an architect by training. He had studied in Augsburg and Munich, Germany, and later practiced in Chicago. In Milwaukee, he made a career as treasurer for the tannery. Finkler appears to have practiced his architectural trade in Milwaukee only twice. He designed a home for his family on Pine Lake, utilizing a very modern German style. His other Milwaukee design was a home for his brother-in-law, Gustav.[31]

Gustav and Anna Trostel

Gustav, who would later become the president of the company, was the oldest of the Trostel children. In 1896, he married Anna W. Bossert. The couple had three children, Erna, Otto A., and Ilse.[32] The home Adolph Finkler designed for them, at 2611 North Terrace, was completed in 1899. According to legend, Gustav preferred another house design, and plans of that home were found when the Terrace home was sold in 1945. However, architect Adolph talked him into building a very traditional German model instead.[33]

When young Gustav purchased his plot of land on Terrace Avenue and Belleview Place, critics speculated that it might be unwise to build "so far out of town." The only nearby signs of humanity were a farmhouse on Summit and the beacon from the North Point Lighthouse, which swept across the open fields at night. The land to the north was low and contained both a swamp and a pond.

During the summer, the children built a raft to cross the water; in winter they skated on the ice. One of the Trostel children recalled moving day as a near disaster. Wagons carrying the family furniture had no trouble negotiating Lake Drive, but once the road ended, it was slow going across the swampy fields to the new home. At one point, the wagon carrying the family piano sank so deeply into the mud that Gustav summoned tannery wagons and horses to come to the rescue—one unexpected benefit of the family business![34]

The home's design was entirely German. With its 28 rooms covering 7,000 square feet, today it is considered one of the finest examples of German Renaissance in the city.[35] The highest-quality materials were used throughout the structure. The precise exterior lines of the house are sheathed in finely crafted slim brown brick with narrow mortar. Punctuating the hand-pressed brick are creamy, cut limestone panels and stained-glass windows. The third-floor exterior features tall Dutch gables and half-timbers inlaid with stucco, all topped by a roof of red terra-cotta tiles. The gargoyles that decorated the outside are gone, but much of the elaborate iron wrought by Milwaukee's master craftsman, Cyril Colnik, remains.[36] The front door grill, with its carved letter "T," still stands.

Few expenses were spared on the interior. Most rooms were finished with oak paneling and black iron. The dining room's wainscoting is six feet tall, and a pair of large carved caryatid figures adorn the sideboard. The living room, or front parlor, is a departure from the heavy oak and bold iron. Here, elaborately enameled woodwork and ornamental plaster decorate the walls and showcase a stone fireplace that extends from floor to ceiling, its firebox lined with onyx slabs. "Above the overmantel mirror is a fine, typical, rococo cartouche supported by a mustachioed man and flanked by a pair of life-sized cherubs."[37] For finishing touches, the Trostels added light-green rugs specially woven in Austria that complemented their more traditional orientals. The house was designed for both gas and electricity and wired for the latter.[38]

The tall Trostel home actually has four floors. There are three bedrooms, an office, and a sitting room on the second floor. The third floor consists of a huge ballroom. For the most part, the children claimed that great space, spinning around the wood floors on roller skates and bicycles when they could not be outdoors. Above the ballroom is an attic for storage.[39]

Hans Liebert, an architect from Germany, worked with Finkler on the design of the Gustav Trostel house. He was the brother of Eugene Liebert, who had at one time worked at the Trostel tannery and became a favorite architect for some of Milwaukee's wealthiest families. Over the years, Eugene Liebert designed homes for such local millionaires as Henry Harnishfeger, John Schroeder, George Brumder, and Fred Kraus. Eugene Liebert's largest and most renowned architectural commission, however, was the lakefront mansion he built for Albert O. Trostel and his wife, Clara Uihlein Trostel.[40]

Albert O. and Clara Trostel

Clara Uihlein was born in Chicago, but her lineage extended to Milwaukee and the Schlitz Brewery dynasty. That success story started with Joseph Schlitz, who was a bookkeeper when August Krug, the owner of the brewery where he worked, died. Schlitz took over management of the establishment and did so well that he won the heart of Krug's widow. Upon marrying her in 1874, he inherited the brewery. A year later, Schlitz returned to the old country to boast about his success in America. Before he left, he wisely made out a will leaving the brewery to his wife's nephews, the six Uihlein brothers, who had emigrated from Germany. He also ensured that the Schlitz name would never be dropped from the brewery. "Dead or alive," wrote Robert W. Wells, in *Yesterday's Milwaukee*, "he had no intention of allowing the name of Jos. Schlitz to perish from the lips of saloon patrons yet unborn."[41] On May 5, 1875, Schlitz perished when his ship ran afoul of some rocks off the southwest coast of England near the Scilly Islands, leaving his name immortalized in Milwaukee history and the brewery in the capable hands of Clara's uncles.[42]

The Schlitz brewery made the six Uihlein brothers very wealthy men. Like the Pillsburys in Minneapolis and the Rockefellers in New York City,

Clara Uihlein Trostel was enormously important to Trostel between the 1930s and the 1950s. She loaned the company money and helped groom her son for leadership.

the Uihleins in Milwaukee became a classic success story. When Joseph Schlitz died, the largest share of stock went to the eldest Uihlein brother, August. Through hard work and good fortune, he amassed a financial empire. When he died in 1907, he was said to be Milwaukee's wealthiest person, and the Uihlein family was estimated to be worth $200 million. All the brothers stayed in the Milwaukee area except Edward, who moved to Chicago. Edward had four children. His son, Edgar, married Paula Huck, a half-sister of Mrs. Marshall Field II, and one of Edward's three daughters, Clara, married Albert O. Trostel.[43]

The Albert O. Trostels had three children, Elinor, born in 1907; Albert O. Jr., born in 1908; and Beatrice, born in 1912.[44] (Elinor married John Notz, and Beatrice married Frederick Weicker. Today, only the Notz family holds Trostel stock.) In 1907, Albert O. and Clara built one of Milwaukee's most famous homes. The press said the house was a showplace from its earliest days. Eugene Liebert modeled it after a German castle. Located at the far end of Lake Drive, the home commanded seven acres and spectacular views over Lake Michigan.[45]

There is no explanation for the location the couple selected, except that Albert O. positioned his family among good company. Only a few blocks north were the summer homes of prominent figures such as brewery baron Valentin Blatz.[46] Clara's cousin, Joseph Uihlein, the eldest son of August, who had married Ilma Vogel (an heir to Pfister and Vogel, the largest tannery in town), rejected the neighborhood near the brewery where the rest of his family was building. Instead he chose to build at 3318 North Lake Drive, just north of the Trostels' lot.

Whether Albert O. was competing with his in-laws and peers or simply seeking the good life, he and Clara clearly built and lived in a showplace. And why not? The business his father had started 50 years earlier was a resounding success, and Albert O. and his brother Gustav, both now firmly entrenched in the family business, could afford such luxuries.

For many years, Albert O. and Clara's home was assessed higher for taxes than any other in the city.[47] The *Milwaukee Journal* called the home "Milwaukee's best known house."[48] The 20-room house was surrounded by acres of manicured gardens and overlooked hundreds of feet of Lake Michigan beach. Its street frontage was 419 feet, and the lot was 1,133 feet deep. In the manner of the times, young Trostel spared no expense. His dining room seated 60 people; the interior was said to contain some of the finest and costliest marble and woodwork in the city.[49] Even in 1927, the mansion was valued at $346,000.[50]

A Nation at War and a Thriving Tannery

On September 1, 1909, with its founder deceased, Albert Trostel & Sons was incorporated with a capital stock of $2.7 million. Gustav was named president, Albert O. was vice president and treasurer, and Adolph Finkler was named secretary.[51] Gustav had a thorough and practical knowledge of the tanning process, so he supervised the factories. Albert O. was said to have executive ability and oversaw the business operations of the company.

The men and their families were prominent community members and active in society. Gustav and Albert O. were members of the Deutscher, a German club that during World War I would change its name in response to public pressure. They were also members of the Milwaukee Yacht Club, located just down the bluffs from their homes, and the Calumet Club. Professionally, they served on the boards of various companies including the Western Leather Company, the United States Glue Company, and the Illinois Leather Company.[52]

The onset of World War I presented Milwaukeeans with conflict, change, and opportunity. Although they had assimilated in many ways, many of Milwaukee's German families were torn between their parents' homeland and their new country. Even after anti-German sentiments began to take hold elsewhere in the United States, Milwaukeeans of German ancestry held fast to their homeland allegiances. In March 1916, they held a rally to aid the German cause. The seven-day bazaar raised $150,000 for war casualties in Germany, Austria, and Hungary.[53] Significantly, Ida Trostel Finkler was featured in a program written entirely in German. The portrait of Frau Adolph Finkler headed a list that included both Trostel wives.[54]

Those actions did not represent the feelings of the entire city, however. That same year, the *Milwaukee Journal* began an editorial series challenging the city's pro-German stance. The work won a Pulitzer Prize for the newspaper three years later.[55] If assimilation had come gradually since German immigration began, the war's impact was quick and noticeable. The names of restaurants and food products were Americanized. In 1917, the Deutscher became the Wisconsin Club. A year later, the German language was made optional in the public schools; by 1919 it was eliminated entirely.

Milwaukee's industrialists, while they may have harbored some sympathy for the German cause, were fully prepared to furnish America's military with supplies needed for the war. Packing plants produced rations for the soldiers; Harley Davidson supplied motorcycles; and machine shops such as Falk, Cutler Hammer, and Allis Chalmers produced gears, drives, electrical controls, and motor controls for military equipment.[56]

The war accelerated the demand for leather and boosted prices of tanned hides. Milwaukee's production rose to $60 million in 1919. The young Trostel men expanded the factory that year, adding a seven-story concrete structure for experimental tanning and warehousing.[57] The company's principals were particularly proud of a special leather product that became well-known during World War I. As a main supplier of leather for the military, the tannery originated the purple Trostan calf, a product whose color became the official hue for all officers' dress boots and was used for fine civilian footwear. As the sole producer of this item, the Trostel company was hailed as one of the preeminent tanneries in the world.[58]

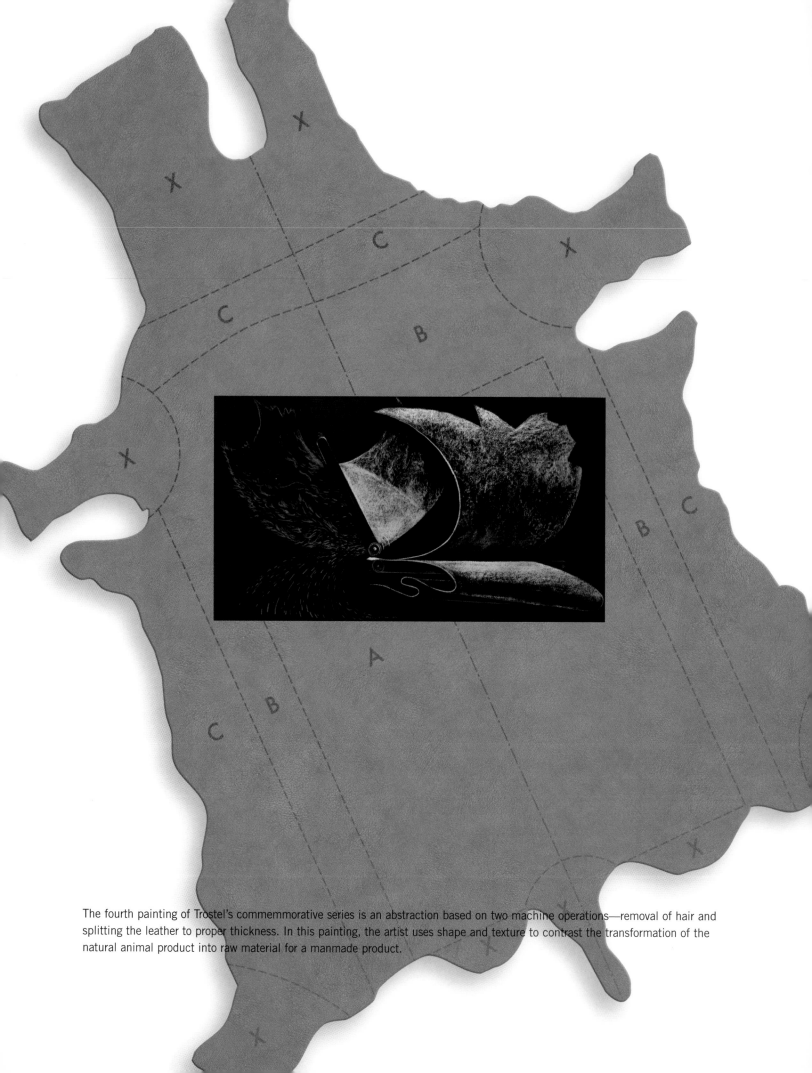

The fourth painting of Trostel's commemmorative series is an abstraction based on two machine operations—removal of hair and splitting the leather to proper thickness. In this painting, the artist uses shape and texture to contrast the transformation of the natural animal product into raw material for a manmade product.

CHAPTER FOUR

THE DEPRESSION AND ITS AFTERMATH

1920 – 1939

Hide output was at an all-time low, and the future was bleak. Yet Albert O. Trostel Jr. brought to the company exactly what it needed at that moment: youthful exuberance, an interest in mechanization and technology, a global perspective, the inclination to plan ahead, and an openness to new ideas.

MILWAUKEE'S INDUSTRIAL economy, prosperous during World War I, gave the city a false sense of security against normal economic ebbs and flows. The decline in war orders for manufactured goods that followed the signing of the armistice in 1918 had minimal effect in Milwaukee. Prices were inflated, and across the country, the demand for material goods rose.[1] Company owners prospered during this period, but the soaring cost of living made life difficult for workers.[2] In time, this unhealthy financial climate created an economic downturn, a slowdown that would have profound effects on manufacturing. In 1920, Milwaukee's leather production fell by 41 percent.[3]

By 1923, however, there were signs that the slump was over.[4] Business gradually improved, and production increased so that in 1928, the *Milwaukee Journal* claimed the city was enjoying its most prosperous time ever.[5] That year, $44 million was spent on building in the city, three-fifths of it for new housing. In March, the employment rate was higher than it had been in five years. The value of products manufactured in the city climbed to more than $1 billion.[6]

The boom times of the 1920s ended with the stock market crash of 1929. Initially, Milwaukee withstood the financial devastation; eventually, it was hit harder than almost any area in the country.[7]

The city suffered enormous declines of employment compared with other cities.[8] Between 1929 and 1933, the number of employed wage earners dropped 75 percent.[9] More than half the city's homeowners were unable to pay their property taxes, leaving the city government unable to meet payroll.[10] Shantytowns, or "Hoovervilles," as they were called, arose in Lincoln Park; homeless men slept in little more than cardboard lean-tos.[11] Unrest led to disorder, with labor unions using sit-down strikes and public marches to press for their employment demands.[12]

Hard Times for Albert Trostel & Sons

At the Trostel tannery, the directors hoped the economy would rebound as it had in the early 1920s, but that would not be the case. The *Milwaukee Sentinel* reported that "by 1931 the company was reeling under the full blow of a slumping economy, and its future was bleak."[13] The earliest remaining records of company meetings date to January 29, 1932. At that time, the heirs of founder

Although the Depression years were a difficult time at the tannery, business would pick up again after Albert O. Trostel Jr. assumed the presidency in 1936.

Albert Gottlieb Trostel were still in charge of the business, in the same positions they had held for the 23 years since the company was incorporated. First son Gustav was president of the company; Ida's husband, Adolph Finkler, was secretary; and second son Albert O. Trostel, who typically presented financial and business proposals, was generally referred to as the treasurer.[14]

Clearly, obtaining money and credit was the order of the day. On March 19, 1932, a special meeting was held to sign corporate papers endorsing Chase Manhattan Bank for loans and credit.[15] Just over a week later, another meeting was held, not at the customary location in the Commerce Street offices, but at the law firm Lines, Spooner and Quarles. There is no record of who called the meeting or what events led to the occasion, but the facts presented in the minutes give a startling picture of the families' financial situation and the desperation of the times.

The three officers present represented their respective families. Importantly, the proceedings also involved the finances of two of the wives, Ida Trostel Finkler, daughter of the company founder; and Clara Uihlein Trostel, Albert O.'s wife and the daughter of the wealthy Chicago industrialist Edward Uihlein. She was also the niece of Edward's brothers, the Milwaukee Uihleins, who were at that time Milwaukee's wealthiest family. It is not clear whom the law firm represented, but there is every reason to believe that Gustav, Ida, and Clara had the most to gain from the outcome.

The minutes carefully detail family members' current accounts with the corporation. Records show that two people were heavily in debt to the company. Adolph Finkler, Ida's husband, owed the company nearly $700,000; and Albert O. had borrowed from the company, through loans, a stocks-and-bonds account, and "open accounts," a staggering sum of nearly $2 million.[16]

At the same time, the corporation was indebted to other family members. Gustav had loaned the company almost $70,000, and Ida had contributed nearly $35,000. But the largest outstanding loan to the company came from Clara, who was related to the Trostels only by marriage but was decidedly a woman of means. Her open account showed the company owed her more than $2.5 million.[17]

An agreement was reached to resolve the families' liabilities and clear the company's books. The minutes mention an attorney present for Clara, perhaps to protect the Uihlein fortune and Clara's assets. Following a discussion, a motion passed unanimously as follows: Albert O. repaid some of his debt, and the remainder was canceled against Clara's loans, leaving a balance owed her of $500,000.[18] Similarly, Adolph's loans were somewhat offset by the amount the company owed to Ida.[19] In addition, Clara and Gustav agreed to use what the company owed them to offset the remainder of Adolph's debt. The remaining amount was written off as a loss on the company books.[20]

Through the agreement, Albert O. and Adolph Finkler were released from their debt. In return, Gustav and Clara forgave the company everything owed them. Finally, and importantly, in the last item on the five-page document, the officers of the company were clearly and strictly "instructed to make no further advances or loans to any officer, director, or stockholder of the company."[21]

Just 20 minutes later, the directors met and used their own votes and the proxies from their families to ratify the agreement. Since the incorporation of the company after founder Albert Trostel's death, each family held 6,500 shares of stock. Over the years, those shares were divided among family members in varying proportions. On March 31, 1932, Gustav voted all 6,500 shares of his family's stock, representing by proxy the votes of his wife, Anna, and the 300 shares held by each of his children: Erna Trostel Read, Otto A. Trostel, and Ilse Trostel Sproule. Albert O. voted his 6,370 shares, and the attorney present for his wife may have voted her 130 shares by proxy. Finally, Adolph voted his 130 shares as well as his wife's 6,370 shares by proxy.[22] On this day, proxy assignments were not pertinent to the voting outcomes, but that would change. Difficult times would continue, but by keeping its financial problems in the family, the company had prevented a major capital crisis from sinking Albert Trostel & Sons. The shareholders' refusal to take the company public would certainly benefit Albert Trostel & Sons again in the future.

The Decline of Albert O. Trostel

In the wake of poor business conditions and personal financial problems, Albert O. began withdrawing from company operations. When the directors met on July 28, 1932, Albert O. was out of town. The company's financial problems had persisted, and that special meeting was held to approve borrowing $20,798 against Gustav's life insurance policy held by Northwestern Mutual Life Insurance Company, in Milwaukee.[23] The next directors meeting was held November 1, the last Albert O. attended as a company director.[24]

On January 4, 1933, Albert O. offered his resignation. His letter was simple and to the point. "For reasons of my own I hereby tender you my resignation as director and officer of Albert Trostel & Sons Company, to take effect as soon as is convenient for you."[25] He went on to say that he would like his son, Albert O. Jr., to succeed

him if the directors agreed. Trostel concluded, "My relations with the company have been most pleasant . . . and it is with a feeling of best wishes for the future welfare of the company that I sever my connections."[26]

Newspaper reports claimed that Albert O. left the company because he was saddened by poor business during the Great Depression. The March meeting the previous year settling Albert O.'s debts with the company pointed to his personal financial difficulties, which continued. Probate records from the time of his death itemize hundreds of thousands of dollars of debt, eventually covered by his

After a 1935 fire destroyed the Trostels' Lake Drive mansion and her husband's death a year later, Clara Uihlein Trostel had this house built. Like Clara, the house was, at once, commanding and respectful.

wife.[27] It is safe to say that Albert's last years were not happy ones.

Nothing is more symbolic of these heartrending times than the destruction of Clara and Albert O. Trostel's castle home on Lake Drive. The mansion, built as a monument to one man's success, was, at one time, the largest and most expensive home in the city, but it fell into ruin in the 1930s, yet another casualty of the Great Depression. The tragedy began with a fire in 1935 that started behind a fireplace faced with Persian tiles illustrating the Goddess of Fire.[28] After the fire, the home was abandoned and sold to demolitionist Frank A. Pipkorn for the incredibly small sum of $500. Pipkorn could not believe his good fortune. He salvaged 500 bottles of wine out of the basement and then sent word that the rest of the home's elegant contents was for sale. Reportedly, actor Gary Cooper's gardener heard about the relics coming on the market from actor Charlie Chaplin's gardener, who had worked for the Trostels. Cooper is said to have wired Pipkorn, "Hold items of value for my observation. Will see you the latter part of next week." Pipkorn purportedly wired back without delay. "Hold nothing. Come quick."[29]

And come they did. The bargain-hunting connoisseurs rushed in from near and far. Newspaper reports say that Gary Cooper bought bricks, and industrialist Henry Ford purchased gargoyles that peered down from the rooftops. Shoe magnate Ralph Weyenberg took stone and glass greenhouse panels to enclose his swimming pool and construct an orchid garden. Robert Friend, of Nordberg Manufacturing, bought 1,200 feet of marble for just a dollar per foot and walked off with a $2,000 vase for which he paid just $500. Royal Lee, a vitamin maker who was building a home in Elm Grove, sought out the carved-stone front doorway, a steal at just $300. For interior bronze doors, he paid $500. Sylvia Graf, of Graf Beverages, purchased the exterior bronze doors for $1,000 and procured all the Tiffany fixtures from inside the home. Watertown native Wayne Miller bought 15 solid oak doors, all the red stone flooring, and the red exterior tiles and roof for less than half their cost. The Grafton hotel lobby installed marble from the recreation room, and walnut bookcases were sent to the State Teachers' College—an institution which later became the University of Wisconsin-Milwaukee.[30]

The Son Also Rises

The directors agreed that Albert O. Jr. should succeed his father as a company director. Gustav Trostel and Adolph Finkler accepted Albert O.'s resignation on January 6, 1933. Albert O. Jr. was elected vice president to fill out his father's term. Gustav remained president, and Adolph's title changed from secretary to treasurer.[31] But Albert O. was not forgotten. The directors honored him at a January 18 meeting, recognizing his contributions as a person who had been associated with the company for so many years. He was given an honorary position as chairman of the board and invited to daily meetings that were set up for an executive committee composed of the directors, three other company executives, and himself.[32]

The period following Albert O.'s resignation was a time of ascendancy for Albert O. Jr. and Clara. First, the stock within their family was reassigned. A year earlier, Clara had held 130 common shares of company stock, and her husband held the family's remaining 6,370 shares.[33] After Albert O.'s resignation, Albert O. Jr. was given his first voting stock, in the amount of 30 shares. Clara took control of 2,600 shares, leaving her husband with 3,870 shares. Clara assigned her proxies not to her husband but to Albert O. Jr., setting the field for a brief but determined demonstration of mother-son teamwork.

Albert O. Jr. joined the company during unsettling times. Three meetings were held before a vote could be held on treasurer Adolph Finkler's annual report.[34] Finally, on February 17, 1933, the treasurer was able to present a report that garnered an approval motion. The motion carried, but for reasons unknown, Gustav made the unprecedented move of voting against its approval. Next, the board voted to accept the actions of the directors since the last stockholders' meeting. Again, Gustav voted against the measure.[35] The minutes do not indicate what details Gustav found objectionable.

Now that her 25-year-old son was the vice president of this large Milwaukee corporation, Clara took action to hone his skills and empower his position. The company had settled its debt to Clara the year before, and the agreement forbade her to make any more loans to the company. But these were difficult times, and the company apparently did not have the funds or the credit to secure calfskin for tanning. Therefore, Clara suggested a way around the agreement, offering to supply calfskin for the tannery to finish. At a directors meeting on July 22, 1933, Gustav, Adolph, and Albert, O. Jr. approved an arrangement whereby Clara would purchase calfskins that she would then turn over to the tannery to finish and sell. The company would take earnings from the tanning and a percentage for handling the sale. Significantly, Albert O. Jr. would have full authority over the tanning of her products, and Clara would have a voice in setting the selling prices.[36]

The next year, Clara—now with a considerable financial stake in company operations and a son in the number-two management position—set forth to improve her corporate standing even further. Her newfound authority came with a realignment of stockholders' shares and an unexpected turn of events in proxy assignments. Part of her power derived from 30 additional shares she had received from her husband. Albert O., who by now was not attending company meetings, had also given 1,370 shares to son Albert O. Jr., along with his proxy for voting. That meant Albert O. Jr. now held 1,400 shares. The surprising change in shareholder-proxy assignment came from within the Finkler family. For reasons that remain unclear, Ida, who had until this time always given her proxy to her husband, Adolph, switched ranks in 1934 and gave 5,643.82 proxy votes to Clara and 726.18 to Gustav.[37] At the 1934 stockholders meeting, Clara exercised her enhanced voting power with conviction.

The fateful meeting was held February 23, 1934. First, the contract with Clara was approved. The minutes noted how the profits were benefiting the company. Then Clara moved that the corporation sell the office and warehouse, a move that was not favored by all the directors. She and her son voted for the measure, assuring its passage. Gustav voted against selling the building. Adolph, reduced to just 130 shares, did not vote. Then Albert O. Jr. raised the subject of increasing the size of the board from three members to five, but that topic was only discussed, not voted upon.[38]

Clara and Albert O. Jr. continued to exercise their authority when the stockholders meeting was reconvened four days later. Proxy votes remained the same. The first matter of business was the sale

of the Commerce Street property. Albert O. Jr. presented a letter to a real estate firm proposing the building's sale. Clara moved the letter be sent. Albert O. Jr. seconded the motion, which carried over the negative votes of Gustav and Adolph.

Next, Albert O. Jr. proposed a resolution raising the number of directors to five. This motion passed unanimously. The company added two directors: Gustav's son Otto, and Clara, the person to whom the company was most indebted for keeping the doors open during the Depression.[39] In April, the company accepted an offer from Milwaukee Lace Paper to purchase the seven-story concrete structure that had been built on Commerce Street in 1919 for experimental tanning and warehousing. The directors unanimously approved the sale and directed $50,000 of the proceeds be used exclusively to pay delinquent taxes.[40]

The following two years were especially hard on the company and the shareholding families. In December 1935, the five directors authorized more borrowing against Gustav's life insurance.[41] Then in 1936, the company was saddened by the death of two of its directors. At a specially called meeting on July 23, 1936, directors Albert O. Jr., Gustav's son Otto, and Clara expressed their regrets at the passing of Gustav Trostel and Adolph Finkler, who had died just 20 days apart in May. The three remaining directors paid tribute to the departed with a minute of silence—"an expression of their great loss and respect for the natural business ability and splendid characters" of both men, who had been officers in the company since its incorporation.

Then Clara and the third generation of Trostels proceeded with business. Albert O. Jr. resigned as vice president and became president, Otto was named vice president, and Clara became secretary for the company she had steadfastly kept in business.[42]

The next recorded directors meeting was held October 17, 1936, this time at the law offices of Lines, Spooner and Quarles. Albert O. Trostel had died on October 14, and this meeting bade farewell to the last of the second-generation Trostels. Noting that he had served the company since its incorporation, the board recognized Albert O. Trostel for "his high character, lofty business ideals, and valued and faithful services to the company."[43] The last order of business would release the young

Trostels from their ties to the second generation: Albert O. Jr. accepted the resignation of his mother, Clara, as board secretary.[44]

Clara's Contributions

After her resignation, Clara Trostel maintained an active involvement in the business. Those who knew her described Clara as delightfully warm, beautiful, and generous, and an energetic force.[45] Her financial contributions saved the company from ruin twice—first by providing millions of dollars of loans knowing full well that not all the money would be repaid, and then by contracting to purchase calfskin for the company to process when its machinery otherwise would have stood idle. Her influence stretches across the entire Trostel history. She married the founder's son, and then groomed her own son for the presidency, but Clara's most lasting personal contribution came when she recommended that the company hire a financial director in 1938.[46]

The young man Clara chose for the position was employed in Milwaukee as a financial analyst in the securities industry and had a good business sense. Everett G. Smith was a Milwaukee native, born January 5, 1909. He attended Milwaukee Country Day High School and graduated from Dartmouth—which he attended with his close friend Albert O. Trostel Jr.—in 1930.[47] At the time Clara chose him to become Trostel's financial manager, Smith was well-positioned in the community as a member of the Towne Club and the Milwaukee Club.[48] To Clara's mind, Smith was exactly what the company needed.

Clearly, she was a good judge of character. Smith would be named treasurer in 1940; he would later run the company and figure heavily in the Albert Trostel & Sons success story during the latter part of the 20th century.

Albert O. Trostel Jr.

When the Depression hit Milwaukee, Albert O. Trostel Jr. was just beginning his years at the tannery, a business that, like most businesses at that time, was in trouble. Fresh out of college in 1931, Trostel had been named general manager at the tender age of 23. In five short years he found himself heading the entire organization.[49] He was understandably reluctant about taking control of the family business at a time when he was relatively inexperienced. To make matters even more difficult, the business was in dismal condition. Hide output was at an all-time low, and the future was bleak.[50] Yet Albert O. Trostel Jr. brought to the company exactly what it needed at that moment: youthful exuberance, an interest in mechanization and technology, a global perspective, a readiness to plan ahead, and an openness to new ideas.

That latter characteristic was exemplified by an experience Albert O. Jr. had three years prior to assuming the presidency. In 1933, the 25-year-old Trostel was in New York attending a leather show when he was approached by an old German who had a few ideas about Trostel leather.

Everett G. Smith joined Albert Trostel in the 1930s as financial manager. Active in Milwaukee society, he was recruited by Clara and groomed for a senior position.

"[The man] told me how lousy our product was and I was intrigued by his frankness," said Trostel. The gentleman was Karl Kuechel, a retired general manager of the Cornelius Heyel Co. tannery in Worms, Germany.[51]

The two men spoke German and struck up a friendship. The conversation was not flattering to Trostel by any means. Kuechel was brutally honest in his opinions.

"He pointed out the pitfalls in some formulations we used," said Trostel. "I spent hours on end with him. He was a very interesting guy and a wonderful person."

Undaunted and even exhilarated by the criticism, Trostel persuaded Keuchel to come to Milwaukee, making him the first in a long line of foreign consultants. When Keuchel returned to the East Coast, he left behind a wealth of knowledge that Trostel used when he took over the presidency in 1936.[52]

Trostel wasted little time getting his feet wet. Reports say he marched onto the plant floor, rolled up his sleeves, and set about educating himself in the tanning processes from the bottom up. He insisted on learning about and knowing how to operate every piece of equipment, a practice he continued throughout his career. Employees said the plant floor was his office. Right up to his death, it was no surprise to find Trostel on the plant floor in his shirtsleeves, supervising operations.[53] Albert O. Jr. had his hands in every detail, mechanical or manual. Apparently, he appreciated youthful participation. In his later years, he boasted about his young staff. Ability, he said, was more important than maturity. In 1951, he

noted, the average age of the plant's superintendents was 30.[54]

Trostel's experience on the floor informed his business approach. Some believe the biggest asset he brought to the company was a decidedly modern approach to industry, especially in the areas of mechanization and technology. He was tremendously interested in and knowledgeable about machinery,[55] and the Trostel tannery became known as an innovative model of industrial efficiency.[56] The company used power equipment whenever possible—conveyor belts transported materials, and conveyor feed machines eliminated heavy lifting.[57]

Technological advancement was accompanied by chemical development. Albert O. Jr., a chemistry major at Dartmouth,[58] predicted that chemistry would one day dominate the tanning industry. With that prospect, Trostel noted, came some great opportunities.[59]

Trostel was also keen on looking abroad for inspiration. Since his schooling in Switzerland, Trostel had never lost interest in world events and global travel.[60] Early in his career he made a practice of bringing foreign expertise to the domestic tanning process. In 1933 and 1934, he focused on what he could learn from highly skilled tanning technicians from Europe.[61] A few years later, in 1939, his travels to Europe positioned the company to secure the lion's share of the tanning business that would emerge after World War II. While abroad, Trostel correctly determined that the unrest in Europe would surely lead to another world war. When he came home, he instructed his company to make strategic innovations that would give it a tremendous business advantage in the years to come.[62]

This painting depicts a workman, after tanning, removing the tanned sides from the drum. These sides are technically now leather, and pictorially they are no longer wrestled with but handled, according to one Milwaukee art critic. This is the fifth painting in the centennial series.

CHAPTER FIVE

WORLD WAR II

1939–1948

After returning from Europe in 1939 and anticipating another world war, Trostel made the decision to switch from tanning calfskin for ladies' purses to side leather, the product that would be necessary for most leather war supplies. When the war came, the company was the leading supplier of leather for American soldiers' combat boots and most of the Russian army's as well.

WHEN THE WAR BROKE OUT, Milwaukee was not divided in its loyalties as it had been during World War I. Instead, the city was determinedly patriotic. Beloved Mayor Carl Zeidler enlisted in the armed forces and lost his life in the Pacific in 1942. Milwaukeeans planted victory gardens, bought war bonds, and rationed their supplies; horses and buggies reappeared on city streets so that more gasoline could flow to the war effort. Soldiers signed up in record numbers.[1]

On the domestic front, the United States faced a critical production challenge that could be addressed only by heavily industrialized cities like Milwaukee. As the 10th-largest industrial center in the nation, Milwaukee was well-prepared to convert its peacetime production to aid the war effort. Homemakers left their housekeeping duties to become machine operators and assembly line workers. Secretaries worked overtime, and businessmen took over any factory job that would expand production.[2] Accordingly, the city's industrial employment grew dramatically. The number of factory workers in Milwaukee County, which averaged 105,000 in 1940, would reach 177,000 by 1943. In 1946, a year after the war ended, local author John Moranz described the situation eloquently:

The events of December 7, 1941, which plunged our nation into the bitterest and most

costly war in the world's history, brought us face to face with a staggering problem. The industries of the country, already producing armament and equipment for half the world, were now called upon to increase their production to previously unheard levels so that our own nation could be girded for the struggle into which we had become embroiled.[3]

There appeared to be no end to the supplies that would be needed in the years of fighting that lay ahead. Every item related to transportation, especially for ships and planes, was in demand, as were arms and ammunition. United States and Allied troops abroad required an extraordinary amount of goods for housing, clothing, food, and medical care. Furthermore, this vast amount of war material was needed in record time. A nation that was once in the business of producing the highest living standard in the world was now faced with producing the goods necessary for its own survival.[4] Again, Moranz helped paint the picture:

Trostel leather appeared in a wide variety of items, from saddles to shoes and even purses. This purse was made from Trostel-produced calfskin leather.

Town & Country

CONGRESS GAITER

MODEL T

CONGRESS GAITER

RISING STAR

MODEL T

Town & Country shoes

in Fleming-Joffe Reptiles...

these proudly bear the Fleming-Joffe label, so you know the quality of the genuine reptile at once. A whirr of wonderful glistening color..note particularly the polished grays. Excellent companions for Fall. Shoes, **10.95** the pair. Bag 12.95 plus tax.

Town & Country
Fleming-Joffe Reptiles

The Milwaukee-made excavating machinery which dug the Panama Canal was now building the air fields scattered over almost the entire world, and the turbines and gears from Milwaukee plants which had powered the ocean liners during peacetime were now providing the "drive" in the naval fighting craft which were hammering relentlessly at our foes and transporting to the four corners of the earth the greatest fighting force the world had ever seen.[5]

Milwaukee was the world's leading manufacturer of several strategic products that would be needed in the war years ahead, for some of which Trostel supplied leather. No other city on the planet produced as many "diesel and gasoline engines, outboard motors, motorcycles, tractors, wheelbarrows and padlocks." Additionally, the city led the nation in the production of "work shoes, milling equipment, leather gloves and mittens," as well as metal products such as bodies and parts for automobiles. The city was also a key supplier of "electrical machinery and equipment, meat and food products, leather and leather goods, chemicals, paints and textile mill products." Milwaukee was also proud of its many foundries and laboratories.[6] The city's industry supplied the military with utility vehicles, explosives, bomb casings, and parts for tanks. Cutler Hammer produced controls for ships and airplanes, increasing its output 400 percent in 1943. Over 70 local companies made parts for the atomic bomb that essentially ended the war in 1945.[7] According to Moranz, the transformation to wartime production took place quickly:

In a matter of weeks after December 7, a seemingly endless stream of these implements of war had started to flow from the assembly lines of factories whose productive wheels were turning night and day. Silk hosiery gave way to parachutes, auto bodies to aircraft engine parts, and from virtually all of the firms producing the heavy durable goods for which Milwaukee was famous came a host of

Opposite: A Town & Country ad for shoes using Trostel leather. Just before World War II broke out, Trostel switched from calfskin to side leather, which made sturdier shoes.

new products such as guns, torpedoes, airplane superchargers, propellers and landing gears.[8]

The annual value of industrial production rose during that time from $750 million to $1.75 billion.[9] Over the course of the war, Milwaukee produced billions of dollars worth of airplane parts, turbines, marine equipment, bombs, shells, airplane refueling units, clothing, shoes, and parachutes, in addition to hundreds of other items for the armed forces.[10] When additional capacity was needed for production, the government funneled hundreds of millions of dollars into Milwaukee for more factories and other facilities.[11]

The Trostel War Effort

Albert O. Jr. was a keen observer of world conditions and made good business decisions based on his insight and foresight. After returning from Europe in 1939 and ruefully anticipating another world war, Trostel made the decision to switch from tanning calfskin for ladies' purses to side leather, the product that would be necessary for most leather war supplies. When the war came, the company was the leading supplier of leather for American soldiers' combat boots and most of the Russian army's as well.[12] In addition to boot leather, Trostel tanned leather for specialized industrial applications. Trostel's knowledge of and interest in machinery likely showed him the potential for these products, which would one day be the bread and butter of the company's business.

Gearing up for wartime production required an influx of capital. The company used lines of credit, sometimes as much as $2 million, to finance its war production contracts.[13] It also sold timberlands in Villas, Iron, and Ashland Counties.[14] Debentures were issued in December 1941.[15] And the company continued to depend on Clara Trostel's generosity. In 1941, she again infused the business with capital. The sale of her timberlands resulted in proceeds that she credited to her account within the corporation and with which she agreed to purchase stock.[16]

At the stockholders meeting held April 16, 1942, the company reported a profitable return from its war production efforts. First, the directors noted a substantial increase in sales over the preceding two years due to side leather production and sales.

Albert Trostel & Sons now produced 15 percent of the side leather in the country.

In 1942, at the height of war production, Frank Fermano, who was new to the Milwaukee plant, was charged with establishing a control system to track the sides as they made their way through the tannery.[17] It wasn't an easy job. "We were tanning some 55,000 sides of leather a week," said Fermano, who worked for Trostel for nearly 50 years.[18] Approximately 90 percent of Trostel's side leather production was used by the military, according to Fermano.[19] The company recognized that it was making an important contribution to the nation's defense and expected something from the government in return—namely, help in obtaining critical materials such as chrome.[20]

Throughout this period, the company was contemplating its first foreign investment. World War II marked the first time since the Civil War that United States industry was concentrated on war production for at least two years running. Circumstances challenged efficiency and productivity of industrial output. The war had extended into the far reaches of the globe, inhibiting world markets' access to raw materials and transportation resources.[21] "These conditions left their first appreciable mark on the [leather] industry's operations in 1940 when one source of supply after another of imported materials was blocked by the downfall of nation after nation as Axis forces advanced."[22] The import situation grew steadily worse as demand rose. The U.S. armed forces and the pressing demands of lend-lease commitments to supply the Allies challenged an industry that was already stretched to its limits. In 1942, the leather industry was working at capacity and was already drawing on inventory reserves; yet the United States had seen only its first full year of war participation.[23]

Like many across the country, Trostel's factory was staffed by women during World War II. When the war was over, most of the women returned home.

Albert O. Trostel Jr. responded in a manner that reflected his global perspective. At the October 14, 1943, board meeting, directors considered trips to Central and South America to explore new sources of materials and production.[24] In August 1944, the company reported that it was negotiating a partnership with a Colombian company.[25] Eventually the venture was finalized and lines of credit were established for the branch company, Curtiembres Tarud Limitada, in Barranquilla, Colombia.[26] The relationship established Albert Trostel & Sons as an international company. Trostel's globalism would be increasingly embraced by company executives well into the next millennium.

Rewards for Wartime Labors

The tannery's enormous investment of time and energy yielded advantages for all the businesses and for the war effort. The army and navy presented the company the coveted "E" award, given for "excellence in performance in connection with the war effort." The award was scheduled for presentation on December 6, 1944.[27] Further, the Trostel company had prospered during the war. Its working capital at the end of the 1942 had risen to $802,000 from just $177,000 at the end of 1941. The company had decreased its calfskin processing while increasing side leather from 10 million feet in 1941 to 15 million feet in 1942. Man-hours worked over the same period soared to more than 1 million.[28] The company's employees justifiably benefited from their heightened war efforts, and in 1946 they began receiving bonuses.[29]

Directors and investors also shared in the postwar largesse. The directors took bonuses beginning in December 1945, with Trostel and Everett Smith receiving $30,000 each. A year later the two men's bonuses amounted to more than $43,000 each; by 1948, the amount had increased to $58,000.[30] In 1944, the company paid its first dividend in 19 years.[31] In time, the company took another step toward sharing its profits when it set up the Albert O. Trostel Foundation, which continued for many years as a benefactor of the Milwaukee community.[32]

Postwar Milwaukee

After World War II ended in 1945, Milwaukee held victory parades to celebrate the outcome and honor the nearly 3,000 Milwaukee men and women who had lost their lives during the conflict. Commemorating that sacrifice, the city built an architectural showpiece that combined a veterans' center, a public memorial, and an art museum.[33]

Looking ahead, Milwaukee and the rest of the nation were faced with the daunting task of retooling their industries for domestic production. Converting "implements of war to the products of peace" was no small order.[34] The survival of the national and local economies depended on switching back to the demands of civilians. According to Moranz, response was notable.

The problems of reconversion were tackled with the same determination as was the challenge imposed by the war and [in 1946], Milwaukee industry [had] almost completely been restored to its peacetime pursuits. The bulk of Milwaukee's war production was the result of greatly expanded activity by existing firms and a manifold increase in the quantity of products which had been made during peacetime, rather than from the addition of a large number of new items to the list of commodities manufactured.[35]

Milwaukee industry had shown great foresight in the midst of its wartime efforts. Even while the conflict was in full force, local industrialists were anticipating the problems of reconversion they would face once the war was over. "We Work for Victory—We Plan for Peace" was the slogan of the city's factories. That strategy, adopted by local leaders, was typical of the kind of forward thinking necessary for the times. "While devoting their very best productive genius to the immediate need, [they] were ever mindful of the fact that the cessation of hostilities would bring repercussions if intelligent plans were not formulated in advance."[36]

This progressive mind-set remained after the war. Fully aware that these new postwar times demanded new ideas and new practices, the mayor of Milwaukee established a nonpartisan group of

Only the right tannage will do it

When the design of the shoe is rugged the leather must conform . . . must have that masculine, out-doorsey appearance, that indefinable something called 'character', which only the finest leathers have.

Yes, only the right tannage will do it—give a leather all these qualifications which are so noticeable in the finished shoe.

In this particular shoe it's Vegetable Antiquity Sides . . . a Trostel leather tanned to do a specific job.

Tannage by **TROSTEL**

Albert Trostel & Sons Company • Milwaukee

March 27, 1948 — LEATHER and SHOES

11

local businessmen to lead in postwar economic revitalization. That group became known as the Greater Milwaukee Committee, and set out to plan and act on behalf of the community's needs.[37]

By 1946, the city's industries employed 135,000, and its postwar production exceeded prewar levels by 25 percent.[38] Nationally, 408 million pairs of shoes had been produced annually during the prewar years. Now, the postwar baby boom—44 new schools were constructed in Milwaukee to meet rising enrollment in the ensuing years—created a demand for 450 million pairs a year.[39] This growing shoe business fueled postwar production for Trostel.

Postwar Trostel

The tannery had prospered greatly during the war years, but it did not rest on that success. Rather, the directors met the future with a three-pronged approach. First, the company determined that its current buildings and machinery were too old and had been fully depreciated. The directors decided to expand capacity for production by purchasing modern buildings, machinery, and other equipment. They also resolved to set up cash reserves. Once again, its privately held status would allow the company to plan for the long term, with-

Opposite: A 1948 ad for Albert Trostel shoe leather. At this time, Trostel was a leading supplier of shoe leather in the United States.

out being driven by short-term shareholder pressures. Its private status would help Trostel weather the inevitable business droughts that lay ahead. Perhaps most important, the company decided to increase spending for research and development, seeking new products, improved production methods, and expanding markets.[40]

The company had first diversified its product lines during World War II, manufacturing leather parts and gaskets for military machinery and vehicles in the 1940s. When the war was over, Trostel noted that not only were the products revenue for the company, but they had become staples of its line.[41]

With mechanical leather clearly part of Trostel's future, the Leather Packings Division was formed in 1946. The company hired Anderson Nichol, a Boston-based engineering outfit, to help with the transition. "They designed some equipment and machines for us," recalled Fermano. "In the latter part of 1946 and the early part of 1947, we started to go into production in a small way. We were making packings for hydraulic jacks, and we were making carburetor cups for automobiles. At that time, all carburetors required a little leather cup that would pump the gas."[42]

The move into mechanical leather parts was a resounding success. Moving even further away from the company's origins, Trostel launched the production of synthetic rubber seals in 1948. That same year, the company reported a major milestone: profits for the preceding year had climbed to more than $1 million.[43] With product development now a company mandate, Trostel's future looked even brighter.

The sixth painting in the series shows the leather as an abstraction of color, thus emphasizing "the triumph of man in adapting nature to his needs." At the top of the painting, cross sections of drums and color vials show the leather beginning to enter the final phases of its transformation into a finished product.

CHAPTER SIX

POSTWAR DIVERSIFICATION

1949–1962

Whenever we came upon a new method or technique of leather-making, we've tried to make it available to others to foster an exchange of information among tanneries for the benefit of the whole tanning business. This was how we expanded, using our own imagination and the common sense and experience of other people.

—Albert O. Trostel Jr.

VISIONARIES WITHIN THE Trostel company never doubted the inevitability of change. As leaders in their industry, Trostel tannery officials were reverent of the past, but they were not bound to leather-making traditions, products, and methods. The tastes of the public and the needs of industry, they had found, were always in flux. If the past had taught nothing else, it was that new times bring demands for new products. Just as harness, saddle, and carriage leather had become a thing of the past, so would other items. While domestic shoe leather was being challenged in the marketplace by leather from South America and Italy, company officials continued the search for new products and maintained an ongoing exploration of new uses for leather.[1]

The company produced leather seals for brake components.[2] When the automobile manufacturers switched to power brakes, Trostel engineered a leather cup seal that worked with the master cylinder to create the necessary vacuum pressure for braking. At the same time, the company began making cups for the hydraulic jack industry. Hydraulic cups were unique in that they were molded leather. The process involved molding a cut of leather between hot elements, trimming the cup, and then using wax to solidify the leather and the form. Ultimately, the leather had to be impregnable to oil and withstand 15,000 pounds of pressure per square inch.[3] The life of leather seals was generally less than 10,000 miles, so they were eventually replaced with longer-lasting synthetic products.[4]

As sales increased, Trostel's business outgrew the Milwaukee facility. In 1952, the company formally expanded and diversified when it incorporated the industrial leather business, moved it to Lake Geneva, Wisconsin, and named it Albert Trostel Packings Ltd. Before long, Albert Trostel Packings Ltd.'s main product line grew to include the manufacture of oil seals, pneumatic and hydraulic packings, and other leather and synthetic products, primarily for the automotive industry.[5]

The Old Lake Geneva

At first glance, Lake Geneva was an unlikely place for expansion. The quiet, green community contrasted sharply with the gritty, industrial atmosphere of downtown Milwaukee. Lake Geneva was a picturesque country site graced with hills, dales, and clear water. Traders and trappers had long heard about this spot. But the first recorded sighting

---

A tannery worker in the Phoenix tannery. Heading into the 1950s, the Phoenix tannery was operating at its peak, supplying fine leather for a wide variety of purposes.

occurred in 1831 when the John Kinzie party happened upon the lake. John's wife, Juliette, was so taken with the environs she recalled approaching Lake Geneva in her book, *Waubon*.

> *Gently swelling hills, lovely valleys, and bright sparkling streams were the features of the landscape. We descended a long, sloping knoll, and by a sudden turn came full in view of the beautiful sheet of water. Bold, welling hills jutted forward into the clear blue expanse, or retreated slightly to afford a green, level nook, as a resting-place for the dwelling of man.[6]*

It was not long before the area became farmland. That, in turn, gave rise to bustling community development. In 1833, once the area Native Americans contracted with the U.S. government to move to Kansas, the land around Lake Geneva was opened to commerce. Logging mills, gristmills, and

woolen mills sprang up. Out of the needs of businesses and their workers grew a village of shops and saloons. Visitors came by horse and buggy for restful, rural holidays.[7]

For its financial livelihood, the city did not take the industrial path to prosperity like its neighbors, Chicago and Milwaukee. Lake Geneva's expected industrial development was blocked by two nearly simultaneous but unrelated events. In 1871, the Chicago Northwestern train began service from Chicago to Lake Geneva, bringing city folks to the bucolic countryside. That same year, the Great Chicago Fire devastated the Windy City.[8] That cata-

A group of Albert Trostel executives gather around a display of the company's leather products. Although shoes and boots were important, industrial products gained prominence throughout the 1950s.

strophe brought scores of wealthy, displaced city dwellers seeking quality, temporary housing while their businesses and homes were being rebuilt. Chicago's exodus turned the little Lake Geneva community into a host to the well-to-do. Families recuperated along the banks of the sapphire waters, while husbands and fathers commuted to the big city.[9] These visitors were accustomed to the finer things in life: quality services, exceptional goods, and superior food. At once, Lake Geneva was transformed from a community that exported goods to one that imported the affluent and tended to their needs.

Over time, living in Lake Geneva for summers or holidays became a way of life for wealthy Chicagoans. On the shores of the lake, extravagant villas and luxurious mansions sprang up and became local attractions. Manicured parks, full-service resorts, and graceful hotels dotted the green hillsides, each establishment grateful for, and owing its survival to, well-heeled patrons. The new citizenry drank in the fresh air and unpolluted waters and basked in the genteel and restful ways of "country life."

The New Lake Geneva

The decision to relocate the industrial leather business to Lake Geneva also reflected on the situation in Milwaukee, the birthplace of the Trostel company. Throughout the 1940s and 1950s, migration from the South to northern industrial cities like Milwaukee changed the socioeconomic and cultural mix of these urban areas. Between 1940 and 1950, Milwaukee's African-American population doubled, and would increase fivefold by 1970.[10] The newcomers did not fully integrate into Milwaukee society, and over time, the city's increasingly segregated society would see social problems, particularly in the downtown area where the Trostel tannery was located.[11]

Yet relocating to a town such as Lake Geneva posed different problems. Long a tourist and vacation destination, Lake Geneva did not invite heavy industry until 1951. Winning the hearts and minds of the locals was necessary before building a plant. This job fell to John Strackbein, a longtime Trostel employee who understood the nature of a proud, small community and was gifted in appealing to its

sensibilities. For starters, Strackbein took on the mantle of a local. He had a deep affection for and believed in Lake Geneva. He was certain that the community would benefit from Albert Trostel Packings. He and his wife purchased a home in town and enrolled their two children in the local schools.[12]

Similarly, when Strackbein began filling positions, he insisted on giving preference to the locals. He was particularly in favor of hiring women. To help people know and understand him and his company, he arranged to have the "in-house" newsletter printed weekly in the *Lake Geneva Regional News*. The piece was at once informative and folksy. Strackbein explained company products and their uses; and he discussed negotiations between labor and management, particularly important considering that the company was nonunion. The newsletter covered employees' community activities, their volunteer efforts, their sports events, the victories and defeats, and all efforts made by company members that contributed to the community welfare.[13]

Once it had been accepted by the local community, Trostel's operation in Lake Geneva was very profitable. The plant occupied 50,000 square feet, employed 350 people, and soon announced an addition to keep up with the growing manufacturing of oil seals, pneumatic and hydraulic packings, and other leather and synthetic products for industry.

There were, however, some labor union problems. On January 29, 1953, machinists in the Lake Geneva plant went on strike. They were demanding a union shop and raises. Three dynamite bombs were detonated, one at the home of Strackbein and two at the homes of two nonstriking employees. Strackbein spoke out, declaring that in its two years in Lake Geneva, the Trostel Company was continually hampered by union activities. So when the union employees went out on strike, Trostel advertised and hired other workers, mostly women, to take the strikers' places in the plant.[14] This move settled the conflict. It would be almost a full decade before Trostel once again ran into union unrest at the Lake Geneva plant.

The Lake Geneva Business

Amid the labor trouble, Trostel Packings enjoyed much success. When the operation first moved from Milwaukee to Lake Geneva in 1952, the company began manufacturing polyurethane.[15] Taking a cue from the technophilic Trostel Jr., the subsidiary's engineers and chemists began exploring potential alternatives to mechanical leather. The original polyurethane product was similar to foam rubber and could be used in cushions, insulation, and insoles for shoes, as well as underpadding for carpets.

Soon, however, the engineers and chemists began working with the sales staff to explore methods of liquid casting, which involved heating the product, then molding and curing it. The resulting product was a rigid form of lightweight elastomer with remarkable industrial strength and highly effective insulation characteristics.[16] It was the ideal product for the drive wheels and pallet wheels on industrial forklifts. It was also effective in cushioning metal-on-metal operations, such as those found in the suspension systems under railcars. Because these applications required completely different expertise from the industrial leather operation, the polyurethane business existed as its own entity within the Trostel organization. In 1957, the Polyurethane Division of Albert Trostel Packings Ltd. was established, and continued to develop and market high-quality urethane products in Lake Geneva.

By 1958, Trostel Packings was a significant U.S. supplier of automobile carburetor cups. At one time, Trostel Packings was producing 25,000 to 30,000 carburetor cups a week.[17]

Finally, in 1959 the Polymer Compounding Division of Albert Trostel Packings Ltd. was created. Trostel had been producing synthetic rubber seals since 1948, when it became apparent that synthetic rubber could be used for a wide variety of industrial applications.[18] The establishment of the division, which would be responsible for formulating and mixing rubber,[19] signified even more diversification.

"We tried everything," remembered Merrill Karcher, who, like many of his colleagues, was a lifer, joining the packings operation in 1955 and retiring 44 years later. "We made cups for oil wells, and then we got into wheels, urethane wheels on lawnmowers, and replacement seals for everything."[20]

All this activity in Lake Geneva was not for naught. In 1960, Trostel Packings was recognized in the local paper. "Trostel [is] one of the nicest things that ever happened to the community," the article read. Since its founding and under Strackbein's

leadership, "it has moved in only one direction—forward." The company has progressed through "expansion of production, markets, labor force and plant, plus the creation of two subsidiary firms. Today, its quality products are known and used throughout the world."[21] The company was recognized for its good citizenry. There were 400 local people on its payroll, with earnings in excess of $1 million.[22]

During this period, the plant floor had increased to 80,000 square feet from 23,000, with three additional leased warehouses. The company had become a large producer of mechanical seals and packings. Seals also were used in farm equipment, washing machines, aircraft, and hydraulic equipment.[23] Sales in 1959 totaled more than $10 million, a 50 percent increase over 1958, which had been 45 percent greater than 1957.[24]

The Tannery in the 1950s

While Trostel Packings was enjoying early success, the parent company suffered a major personal loss. On October 1, 1956, Clara Uihlein Trostel died in a Milwaukee hospital, just a few hours after her brother, Edgar J. Uihlein, passed away in Chicago.[25] Clara had rescued the company from financial difficulties and even potential disaster. Further, she had prepared her son for the company presidency and ensured his ascendancy. In a tribute to his mother's life, Albert O. Trostel Jr. praised her "valued counsel" as a principal stockholder and businesswoman. "Without her financial aid the company could not have survived," read a board resolution.[26]

Her son now had 20 years on the job and a sizable family of his own. He and his wife, Kendrick, were the proud parents of three daughters—Janet Orr, Clara Louise, and Tara Kendrick—and a son, Albert O. Trostel III, who ultimately earned a chemistry degree from Cornell and a postgraduate degree from MIT.[27]

Despite his veteran status, Albert O. Jr. still reported spending about 90 percent of his time on the plant floor, and he continued to be a major force with the company.

"My training in the tanning business was nil," Trostel said. "First I had to learn the business and the best way seemed to be able to do the actual work."[28] He spent so much time on the floor, his son recalled, that he began to resemble the tannery in a rather unpleasant way. "In the late '50s," said Trostel III, "my younger sister walked into the tannery, and her nose went up in the air, and she said, 'It smells just like Dad.'"[29]

Yet Albert O. Trostel Jr. also found time for other pursuits. In addition to spending time with his family, he served on community boards, including those of the University School, the Community Chest, Red Cross, Curative Workshop, and Columbia Hospital. He was a member of the Greater Milwaukee Committee's Aviation Committee. When time allowed, he enjoyed hunting and fishing.

The tannery made great progress during Albert O. Trostel Jr.'s 25 years of leadership. It was the city's largest tannery and one of the major producers of side leather in the world. By the 1950s, Trostel had modernized and streamlined operations to the

point that it took only two days to process the equivalent of an entire month of leather production in 1931.[30] He had also pushed the company to prepare for the peacetime economy after the war, when the tannery supplied the country's major shoe producers with leather.[31]

Trostel later said he was able to increase production capacity 12-fold in 20 years by switching to power equipment, conveyor belts, and gravity feed, pouring dyes into coloring drums through holes in the ceiling to avoid manual lifting. These improvements enabled the company to increase production from 5 million square feet of hides a

Workers in the Milwaukee tannery handle pallets of hides. These hides were later used for shoe leather and various industrial applications, including seals and gaskets.

year to 60 million, which is the equivalent of 30 million pairs of shoes. During this time of greater production efficiencies, the plant space was cut in half.

Higher production meant more byproducts. Always on the lookout for new ideas, in 1952 Trostel hired Charles Koch, an experienced engineer, to find markets for tanning byproducts. Dubbed "Charlie Garbage" by his fellow workers, Koch was extremely inventive.

"I specialized in what they called offal, or tannery side products," Koch said. "We used cattle hair, for example, for the old-fashioned padding for carpeting. It was called a waffle weave."[32]

Other byproduct uses abounded. Initially, hide trimmings were sold to a glue company. Trostel determined it might be wise for the company itself to manufacture glue and perhaps other products. Koch spent $50,000 for a redwood tub and purchased a patent to allow the trimmings to be processed. The company then hydrolyzed the byproduct with phosphoric acid and reduced it in the redwood tank. The product could be sold as protein. It was also hydrolyzed into a grease that was purchased by the Colgate Palmolive Company and used for food processing.

Above: A Trostel employee preps hides for the next step in the tanning process. The plant's efficiency steadily increased throughout the 1950s until it took only two days to accomplish what formerly required a month in the 1930s.

Opposite: Tannery workers in the Milwaukee tannery in 1952.

An equally important Trostel innovation was the significant use of practical chemistry. His plant was one of the few in the nation to house its own on-site control laboratory and staff it with 10 technicians. "[Chemistry] will make greater contributions in the years ahead," Trostel declared. "These contributions will give the tanning industry great opportunities."[33] Known as a leader in technical advancement, the company prided itself on sharing its knowledge. Trostel explained:

Whenever we came upon a new method or technique of leather-making, we've tried to make it available to others to foster an exchange of information among tanneries for the benefit of the whole tanning business. This was how we expanded,

*using our own imagination and the common sense
and experience of other people.*[34]

Trostel's frequent trips beyond Milwaukee made travel a fixture in the organization. Trostel figured that he was out of town at least one day of the week, routinely traveling to visit customers and suppliers. To ease the difficulties of travel and streamline the time involved, the company formed a subsidiary, Trostel Aviation. Albert O. Jr. had a special fondness for aircraft[35] and purchased two twin-engine planes for his and other company officials' travels. The planes also allowed the company to rush orders of goods to customers.[36]

The 1950s were important years in other ways—new leadership was on the rise. On September 29, 1953, with Albert O. Jr. in Europe, Everett G. Smith, who had been named executive vice president in 1951, conducted his first meeting.[37] Board minutes from December 1954 noted that competition in the shoe industry was as severe

as it had been in 20 years. The company was maximizing its yields. New washing and drying systems for cattle hair were installed so it would be acceptable to the American Hair & Felt Company.

Trostel had improved its position in a highly competitive market, increasing production foot per man, from 30.07 in 1954 to 35.09 at the beginning of 1955 and 36.87 by July 1955. The company that year also added its last building to the Milwaukee complex, bringing the total to 22.[38]

Trostel Celebrates 100 Years

In 1958, Albert O. Trostel Jr. was a celebrated man. The year marked his 25th wedding anniver-

---

To ferry executives and satisfy Albert O. Trostel's personal fascination with aircraft, the company founded Trostel Aviation, which operated two twin-engine aircraft.

sary, his 50th birthday, and the centennial of the Albert Trostel & Sons tannery.

The yearlong festivities were enjoyed at the 1776 Commerce Street plant on the west side of the Milwaukee River. Across the river at 1818 North Water, employees at A. F. Gallun & Sons Corp. were also celebrating. That 100-year-old company, founded when partners Trostel & Gallun parted ways a century before, had likewise endured. The two companies exchanged invitations and shared events, enjoying their mutual endurance and prosperity.[39]

The kick-off event of the tannery's centennial celebration was held February 15, 1958, at the new Milwaukee Art Center. There, Trostel unveiled commissioned artwork by Franklin Boggs, the head of the art department at Wisconsin's Beloit College. "The art of tanning has never escaped the tanner walls, but it has now," Trostel told the crowd. "There is beauty around us daily, but we're so used to it, we never see it. Now we can."[40]

Boggs painted a nine-panel series depicting the process of turning the skin of a steer into shoe leather. "The paintings have an enduring message

Above: Everett Smith (left) discusses the seventh in a series of nine paintings commissioned by Albert Trostel & Sons to commemorate the company's centennial.

Below: In 1958, the company celebrated its 100th anniversary. During that century, Trostel had grown into one of the largest tanneries in Milwaukee and a major supplier of side leather.

THE ART WORLD RESPONDS

AT A TIME WHEN THE FREE-THINKING ART society was first exploring a relationship with traditional commercial industries, Trostel's commissioned work did not go unnoticed. *Milwaukee Journal* art editor Frank Getlein's 1958 review of the paintings touched on both their artistic and their symbolic meanings.

The series represents the triumph of man over nature. Color starts out, in a big, bloody composition of the slaughterhouse, as nature's, with the red and white carcass dominating the picture,

and with the skinner's posture and movement following the structure of the dead beast.

As the hide is progressively trimmed, soaked, shaved, tanned, colored, stretched, dried and cut up for shoes, color and line in the paintings echo the transformation of nature into manufactured material.

The blood red of the slaughterhouse dims into beige and yellow, then to blue and gray. In the second half of the series, color brightens up again, but it is now artificial color.

Likewise, the curve of strength in the original steer disintegrates as the series progresses. By midpoint, man's movements are literally aesthetically shaping the hide, instead of the other way around, as in the beginning.

As the negative center of a bright arrangement of colored hides hung up to dry in one

picture, a portrait sketch of Albert O. Trostel, Jr., the tannery president, appears. This is the point at which prudence too often conquers integrity in artists at work for industry.

Not Boggs!

Trostel appears as a point of rest in the volume of color and form in the drying room. He also sums up, symbolically, the whole process of man molding nature. In short, to get into the series, even the president pays his way, artistically.

Milwaukee, as much as any city in the country, has witnessed in the last decade a great flowering of art working for industry.[1]

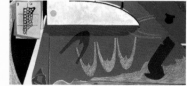

which will last over many decades," Mayor Frank Zeidler enthused.[41] *Milwaukee Journal* art editor Frank Getlein lavished praise on the works. The series symbolized the relationship between art and industry, he wrote. It focused on man's impact on both, and vividly demonstrated how color and form take on meaning for themselves.[42]

The works were exhibited locally before moving to the New York Tanners Council Meeting on February 25. Trostel expected the oils would be displayed permanently in Cincinnati or Lowell, Massachusetts, locations of major leather institutes.[43]

Changing with the Times

As a new decade dawned, the Trostel tannery in Milwaukee was not only one of the largest processors of side leather in the world, it was also Wisconsin's largest tannery of any type. "We were a very successful tannery in our prime," said Anders Segerdahl, a Swede who had apprenticed at Trostel in 1948 and then joined the company in 1956. In 1961, the 103-year-old company employed 850. Of those, some 250 workers had been with the firm 10 years or longer, and the company had not had a major layoff in 20 years.[44]

The economics of the leather business were beginning to change, however, and not favorably for Albert Trostel & Sons Company. Most alarmingly, the South American leather industry was beginning to mature. Earlier, countries like Argentina exported crust, or essentially unfinished leather. By the early 1960s, however, Argentinean companies were beginning to move into advanced tanning

The cafeteria in the tannery building. Albert Trostel was not a unionized shop in the 1950s, and it ran one of the most employee-friendly tanneries in the business.

and finishing. The impetus for this shift came from experienced German and Italian tanners and leather manufacturers who had immigrated to South American countries. The South Americans learned from the Europeans quickly. "They were very good at it," said Segerdahl, who was then head of hide buying and exports in Milwaukee.[45]

The Trostel tannery, headed by men who understood international business, had been quick to try out unfinished leather from South America, and Trostel management had been among the first to import crust from Uruguay. Yet Trostel's leaders could see that finished leather from South America would someday jeopardize the American industry. "We could definitely see that we would have stiff competition in the future," said Segerdahl.[46] South American companies could also produce high-quality leather cheaper, leading to a fundamental reorganization of the American leather industry.

There were other concerns for the Milwaukee operation, too. The tannery needed extensive capital upgrades, even at a time when money was tight due to South American competition. Segerdahl

estimated that the tannery needed about $2 million worth of upgrades.[47] Finally, the neighborhood around the Trostel tannery was beginning to deteriorate further due to urban blight.

Moving to Milan

It was under these circumstances that Trostel expanded its leather operations outside of Wisconsin for the first time, into the community of Milan, Tennessee. Labor was cheaper in the South, and the leather finishing plant was close to some of Trostel's major clients. For its part, Milan had faced severe unemployment problems and welcomed new industry with great enthusiasm.

In July 1960, the city of Milan financed the building of a rubber-molding plant. The city built

The Trostel centennial was celebrated on the outside of the company's tannery building, as well as with a year's worth of parties and events, including the unveiling of a commemorative series of paintings showing the tanning process.

ONE HUNDRED YEARS OF GLOBALISM, PROGRESSIVISM, AND TRADITIONALISM

IN 1958, ALBERT TROSTEL & SONS CELE-brated its 100th year. Throughout its first century, company leaders had not strayed far from the themes of thinking globally and progressively, while honoring founder Albert Gottlieb Trostel's values.

Globalism would prove the most influential of these themes. From its onset, there was nothing provincial about Trostel. The elder Trostel came to America with a healthy world perspective. He had fled the rigid economic controls in Germany and must have relished the freedoms of his new country.

Future generations of Trostels adopted his worldview. Young Gustav went to Germany to study the tanning business; his nephew Albert O. Trostel Jr. also studied in Europe. The company was an active supplier of military products throughout the world and made a very early venture into overseas manufacturing with the joint venture in Colombia beginning in 1944. Global in philosophy and in practice, company officials based their product lines and plant locations on an expansive worldview.[1]

Progressivism was the second hallmark of company operations. Through historic upheavals and market fluctuations, officials embraced the forces of change; they even forecast them. A willingness to diversify, find new products, and open new plants kept the company alive when more provincial and backward-looking organizations might have perished.

The third pillar of Trostel's operation embraced traditional values such as integrity, intelligence, and respect. Holding firm to those core values in light of diversification was key to the company's success. Yet maintaining that balance required an assembly of leaders and workers, people of fortitude and talent who rose to the occasion. The baton had been passed down through three generations of Trostels before Albert O. Trostel Jr. handed it to his good friend and colleague, Everett G. Smith. These were traditional men who were intrigued by innovation, and they set the tone for their employees, as well as for future generations of employees.

the 83,000-square-foot plant for $400,000. In anticipation of company expansion, Milan passed a bond referendum in the amount of $750,000 before the company ever opened its doors.[48]

The much-heralded opening featured a high-profile keynote speaker, Senator Estes Kefauver, who was recognized as a great contributor to the rebuilding of the downtrodden community.

The plant received 1,300 applications for only 300 expected openings.[49] It opened for business in January 1961 with just 35 employees who began the production of synthetic rubber O-rings.[50]

Moving leather operations to Tennessee posed other problems for Trostel. The company had essentially moved work to a nonunion plant. From a corporate viewpoint, unionization was not a major reason for expanding in Milan. From the view of Milwaukee's unions, however, the issue loomed larger, and Trostel was soon accused of moving union jobs out of town.[51] This charge wouldn't hold up under the scrutiny of time, however.

In nearly a decade, the Lake Geneva packing operation had grown into a solid business with great potential. Although leather seals were beginning to be replaced by rubber and urethane, Trostel had good relationships with customers and the ability to move out of leather into more modern elastomer molding.

Eagle Ottawa Steps In

During this time of concern about the Milwaukee complex and the looming competition of imports, Trostel's management was approached by Eagle Ottawa Leather Company, a Michigan tannery. The initial contacts were related to contracts and sales that Milwaukee might handle for the Michigan company. But before long, Trostel executives realized that Eagle Ottawa was actually looking for a buyer.[52] Segerdahl remembered:

They were in a very poor financial situation. They were half in the furniture business and automobile business, and half in the shoe business, primarily specialty leathers, waterproof work shoes and hunting boots and things like that. They had, in those days, a capacity of about 7,000 or 8,000 hides, and I think Mr. Trostel, Mr. Smith, and I became extremely interested because of the automotive and the furniture business.[53]

With Trostel's approval, Everett Smith began negotiations, and an acquisition was finalized in

1961. During the previous decade, Eagle Ottawa had purchased another established tannery, New Jersey-based Blanchard Brothers and Lane, which would now provide Trostel with advanced technical capabilities.

However, technical prowess hardly factored into the decision to purchase Eagle Ottawa. "Eagle Ottawa wasn't doing very well, but it was at the time when people became enamored with leasebacks," said Albert O. Trostel III, who started working for Trostel in 1958. "We ended up selling the whole plant and leasing it back. It was a very expensive purchase, but it raised all kinds of capital."[54] This capital was also invested in the Milan leather finishing plant.

The Death of Albert O. Trostel Jr.

Albert O. Trostel Jr. had always embraced change. New ideas, products, and technology were crucial to the company's success during his tenure as president and would continue to be so in the future. Sadly, just as the company really began to expand and diversify with new plants and the Eagle Ottawa acquisition, Albert O. Jr. died unexpectedly on February 2, 1962, at the Abbott Hospital in Minneapolis, Minnesota, shortly after undergoing vascular surgery to improve his circulation. A board meeting was held on February 19, 1962, in the wake of Trostel's death. According to the minutes, board members offered praises for Trostel that were heartfelt and numerous. Among them was Everett Smith, who was named president of the company a few days later.

Mr. Trostel became president of the company, said Mr. Smith, when it was a small firm on the verge of financial disaster. Through his dynamic abilities, it has become an industry leader. He

Opposite: The *Grand Haven Daily Tribune* ran the acquisition at the top of page one. The paper assured Grand Haven residents that Eagle Ottawa would remain a local firm.

Left: Representatives from Trostel & Sons display a sample of industrial leather seals produced by the company at its Lake Geneva plant. The seals were used in car engines.

Tribune Want Ads Are Inexpensive and Get Results

GRAND HAVEN DAILY TRIBUNE

T Weather

RAIN; WARMER

F report on page 2.

Serving Grand Haven, Spring Lake, Ferrysburg, Fruitport and North Ottawa County — "Where Three Waters Meet"

GRAND HAVEN, MICHIGAN, FRIDAY, APRIL 14, 1961

10 PAGES

Price, Seven Cents

Vol. 76, No. 235

Trostel Industries, Inc. Buys Eagle Ottawa Firm

The Eagle Ottawa Leather Co. sale announcement was made today.

Operations of the 76-year-old firm will continue in the city as a subsidiary of Trostel Industries, Inc. of Milan, Tenn.

Julian B. Hatton Jr. is to continue as president of Eagle Ottawa Leather Co. that is to retain its corporate identity and present management. Sale negotiations were underway several months.

Albert O. Trostel Jr., president of Trostel Industries, Inc., said today, "The only change we intend to accomplish is extensive expansion of the operations of this

highly regarded company."

All present officers of the tannery will continue under the new ownership.

COMMENTING on the sale this morning, Hatton said, "I think it is a good thing for our firm and Grand Haven — to become related to a much larger organization to give more strength to the operation."

The announcement ended months of speculation about one of the city's largest industries that is employing 220 presently and 86 at a second plant at Hackettstown, N.J.

FINANCIAL DETAILS of the complete acquisition of all the stock of Eagle Ottawa Leather Co. were not disclosed. Announcement of an option to purchase was made March 23.

Trostel Industries, Inc., opened a new tannery at Milan, Tenn., near Memphis, a month ago and employs 200 there.

Albert O. Trostel Jr., 52, of Milwaukee is president of Trostel Industries, Inc. of Milan and the 193-year-old Albert Trostel and Sons Tannery at Milwaukee. He also is chairman of the Albert Trostel Packings Ltd. of Lake Geneva, Wis., a leading manufacturer of mechanical seals and packings.

THE TENNESSEE plant has a leather finishing operation and

produce mechanical seals and packings in the 85,000-square-feet new plant.

Eagle Ottawa will continue to produce automobile and furniture leathers, shoe and mechanical leathers. The Hackettstown plant, acquired two years ago, is engaged in fine finishing.

The Milwaukee tannery of Trostel employs 600 as the largest tanner of side leathers in the world. Trostel Industries is a closely-held family corporation.

EAGLE OTTAWA was founded by the late William Hatton whose family has controlled the operation through three generations. Julian B. Hatton Jr. became president when his father, Julian B. Hatton Sr., was killed in a taxi crash on U.S.-16 in 1950.

Sprawling buildings of the Eagle Ottawa Leather Co. plant, Fulton and Beech Tree, are shown in this Tribune aerial photo. The beamhouse, where the hides are tanned, is shown in the foreground along the river.

continually brought new ideas to the business, expanding its involvement throughout many areas. He dealt personally with the company's problems on every level. Everyone who knew him felt respect and warm affection for him.[55]

Mr. Smith voiced the common view of each director that they would attempt to continue the business of the company in the same manner and in the same spirit that existed when it prospered under the leadership of Mr. Trostel. All of the directors expressed the difficulties of carrying on without Mr. Trostel, but pledged their best efforts to the company.[56]

RESOLVED, that the Board of Directors expresses its sense of profound loss upon the death of Mr. Albert O. Trostel, Jr., president of the company and one who embodied the qualities of a great businessman and an understanding friend; that the directors are aware of the great problems which face the management of the com-

pany without the leadership of Mr. Trostel; that the directors will strive to develop the business in the same way that it grew under the gifted guidance of Mr. Trostel.[57]

Many recalled Trostel's history with the company. Frank Fermano, who joined the company in 1936—the same year Trostel assumed leadership—remembered Trostel as "aggressive and very innovative,"[58] characteristics that belied the judgment of some that he was merely a scion.

"Everyone thinks I started out with a silver spoon in my mouth," said Trostel, "but it certainly didn't taste like silver to me."[59] In the 1930s, the company was in the throes of the Great Depression and its survival looked unlikely. But the company managed to weather its most difficult times and survived to celebrate its 100th year, thanks in large part to Albert O. Trostel Jr.

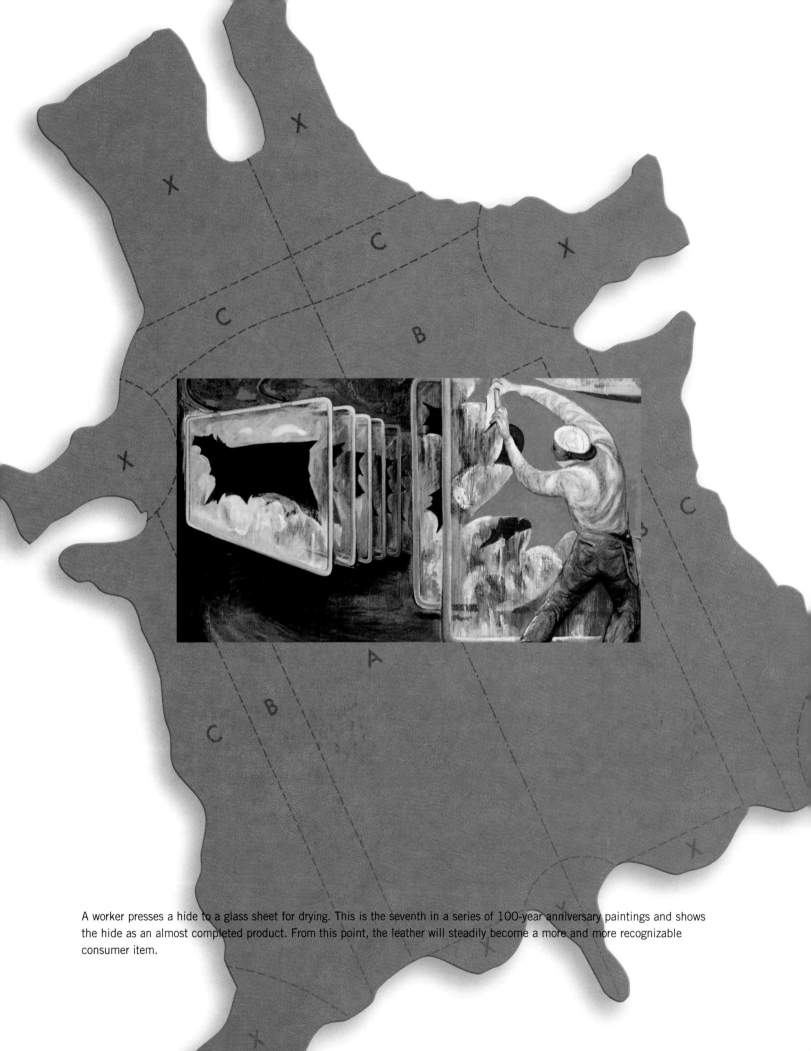

A worker presses a hide to a glass sheet for drying. This is the seventh in a series of 100-year anniversary paintings and shows the hide as an almost completed product. From this point, the leather will steadily become a more and more recognizable consumer item.

THE END OF AN ERA

1962–1969

We came to the realization that the primary product that we historically had made was no longer viable in a U.S. manufacturing facility. Therefore, the decision was made to close the Milwaukee tannery in 1969. We laid off over 900 people.

—Charles Krull

AT THE TIME OF ALBERT O. TROStel Jr.'s death in early 1962, the company maintained the Milwaukee tannery, which primarily used heavy domestic leather and even some imported hides from South America to produce work shoes.[1] But it had begun to expand and diversify in response to fundamental changes in the industry. Between the finishing plant in Milan, Tennessee; Eagle Ottawa, the new acquisition in Grand Haven, Michigan; and the mechanical packings operation in Lake Geneva, Wisconsin, Trostel bore less resemblance with each passing year to the company Trostel Jr.'s grandfather had established more than a century earlier.

Trostel Packings

The oldest of Trostel's subsidiaries, Albert Trostel Packings Ltd., had been producing seals and industrial leather items since the end of World War II. When Everett Smith was appointed to succeed Albert Trostel Jr., John Strackbein, president of Trostel Packings, was promoted to vice president in charge of manufacturing at all Trostel subsidiaries. In 1963, while traveling in Europe, Strackbein suffered a heart attack and died. Frank Fermano, who was with the Trostel Packings subsidiary since its inception, assumed the presidency. Trostel Packings, Fermano

recalled, was producing 90 percent leather items and 10 percent rubber upon its relocation to Lake Geneva in 1952.

In automobiles, the wheel seals were all made out of leather at one time. A leather flange was enclosed in metal, and they crimped that over. A spring surrounded the lip of the leather. The life of the leather seals—10,000 miles—was a lot.[2]

Although leather seals were rather impractical, Trostel's seals had a brush with fame, recalled Merrill Karcher.[3]

Years back, I got a call from a guy, and he said, "Hello, this is Craig Breedlove. I need some low-friction seals for my racecar." We had this seal campaign going—red silicone on the leather seals, so it would be low-friction. He set the land-speed record. Finally, our sales department got ahold of him, and he gave us some testimonials. We used him in our advertising.[4]

Eagle Ottawa was purchased by Trostel & Sons in 1961. At the time, it sold leather to a wide variety of industries, including the furniture upholstery market.

Over time, Fermano said, synthetic rubber would supplant leather in automotive-seal manufacturing.

With the synthetics ... you would stamp the metal casing—just a cup lining—with a hole in the middle. You had to prepare that metal by removing all the oils ... and applying a coat of cement. Then you would mold the rubber right through that metal, and it would be in the shape of a seal. The success of [synthetic rubber] was far greater than [leather].[5]

With its multiple product categories and locations, Albert Trostel & Sons began to decentralize out of necessity. "For awhile, we bought leather from the tannery," recalled Fermano, "but then, when we went from leather to rubber seals, we were on our own. We ran the operation with some direction from [Milwaukee], but not much because we had to go out and find the business."[6]

"We were always successful," added Fermano, who had his own engineering and sales departments. "We ran a pretty good operation."[7] But success would come at a cost as Albert Trostel & Sons remained focused on the old tannery business in at least one crucial way—use of capital.

"Part of our problem back in the '60s was the fact that the tannery was hurting," Fermano said.

"It was difficult for us to get any money for capital expenditures because we were sending all our profits to Milwaukee."[8]

Albert O. Trostel III, who joined the packings subsidiary in 1969, agreed.

By 1968, Packings had been starved of capital. They were making money, but when you started getting under the surface, there were just so many things. We were trying to make molded products for Whirlpool, and 50 percent of the cavities would be damaged.[9]

Eagle Ottawa

The Albert Trostel Packings Ltd. subsidiary somehow profited without an infusion of cash. Meanwhile, at least initially, it was business as usual for Eagle Ottawa in the years following Trostel's acquisition. Purchasing operations were kept separate from Trostel's, as well they should, considering the fact that the Grand Haven,

---

To meet market demands, Trostel Packings continually changed the material it used to manufacture seals—from leather and synthetic rubber to urethane and thermoplastics.

CHAPTER SEVEN: THE END OF AN ERA

The Eagle Ottawa plant in Grand Haven, Michigan. Eagle Ottawa was in financial trouble when Trostel bought it. *(Photograph by Joel Spykerman of Photographic Concepts.)*

Michigan-based tannery used different raw materials than the Trostel tannery.[10]

Julian B. Hatton Jr., who had become president of Eagle Ottawa after his father was killed in a car accident in 1952, stayed on as president, struggling to resuscitate a company that had suffered in the wake of vinyl's rise as an automotive upholstery alternative. "That was, of course, a very serious threat to the future of the company," remembered Hatton Jr.[11]

In response, Hatton directed his company to pursue water-resistant leather technology. Eagle Ottawa wasted no time in drastically altering its tanning processes and applying silicone to its products.

"In the 1960s, I went in the military market and developed, with a [boot] manufacturer, the Vietnam War boot," Hatton remembered. "Boots used by the American Army in the Vietnamese war were made with Eagle Ottawa leather. The top of the boot was a synthetic soft mesh, but the foot part of the boot was Eagle Ottawa leather."[12]

Change was afoot as well. Trostel began to take a more active role in Eagle Ottawa's business; in 1966, by unanimous consent of the board of directors, the wholly owned subsidiary was merged into Albert Trostel & Sons. Moving corporate offices from Michigan to Milwaukee made Eagle Ottawa subject to Wisconsin laws. At the same time, Smith was elected CEO of Eagle Ottawa, while Hatton remained president and traveled frequently between the two companies.[13]

"I had a diesel station wagon, and I would always say that a drive to Milwaukee was a six-cigar drive," said Hatton Jr., who was grateful for the attention from headquarters despite the long trips. "The communications were constant. I didn't feel left alone at all, and I'll never forget that."[14]

The Tannery Closes

While Albert Trostel & Sons welcomed new companies and divisions to the corporate family, the Trostel tannery—the company's meal ticket

THE HISTORY OF EAGLE OTTAWA

EAGLE TANNING WORKS, AS IT WAS then known, was founded in 1865, just a few years after Albert Gottlieb Trostel arrived in America. From its tannery in Whitehall, Michigan, the company initially produced items for the horse and buggy trade.[1]

Eagle Tanning Works was capitalized January 7, 1896, with $150,000 of stock divided into shares of $100 each.[2] Meanwhile, Metz Leather was being organized in nearby Grand Haven. In 1885, the name was changed to Grand Haven Leather Company, and in 1900 its assets were acquired by Eagle Tanning Works.[3]

By 1910, tanneries were finding that the demand for leather associated with horse-drawn transportation was on the decline. Eagle also produced some shoe and boot leather, but its proximity to Detroit and the emerging auto industry provided an even bigger opportunity.[4] Automobile production had come to Michigan largely due to the influence of the banking industry at the turn of the century. The lumber industry in Michigan was declining sharply at that time, giving bankers reason to worry that the decline would be accompanied by a sharp decrease in the demand for loans. So Michigan bankers persuaded automobile companies to set up shop in Michigan.[5]

In 1910, the Eagle tannery name was changed to Ottawa Leather Company, and William Hatton was named manager. In 1916, when the Whitehall and Grand Haven operations merged, the company's name was changed once again, this time to Eagle Ottawa Leather Co., and Hatton was promoted from manager to president.

In 1916, Eagle Tanning Works of Whitehall was combined with the Ottawa Leather Company to form what is now the Eagle Ottawa Leather Company. At that time, the company began its long association with the automotive industry. Under Hatton's leadership, Eagle Ottawa became the largest producer of upholstery leather in the world. Diversification became a specialty as the company branched into leather for furniture, shoes, luggage, book bindings, sports equipment, assorted novelties, valve packings, and other industrial products.[6]

When William Hatton retired in 1936, his son, Julian Hatton, began managing the company. In 1944, Julian oversaw the sale of the Whitehall plant to the General Shoe Corporation.[7] Then, in its most important move during the 1950s, Eagle Ottawa purchased another established tannery, Blanchard Brothers and Lane, of Hackettstown, New Jersey. The purchase provided Eagle Ottawa with advanced technical capabilities.[8]

During these years, Julian Hatton began grooming his son, Julian Hatton Jr., to lead the company. While he entered the tanning business at the insistence of his father, Julian Hatton Jr. was well-prepared. Summers would find Julian Jr. working in the plant, learning the leather-making process. He went to college, and in 1950, returned to Grand Haven with an MBA from Harvard. Because Julian Jr. was already familiar with the tanning process, his father immersed him in sales. Young Hatton was sent around the country visiting sales offices and learning the territories.[9]

Sadly, Julian Jr.'s training was cut short. Just as he was learning the ropes as general manager, young Hatton's father was killed in an automobile accident, a tragedy that plunged the son into the unexpected role of president at the tender age of 27. Hatton remembered the shocking experience of having to learn everything at once, including maintaining his father's legacy. Just two weeks after his father's death, the Republican Party came calling, and members told Julian Jr. that his father had been the best Ottawa County Republican Party chairman in the organization's history, a position now delegated to him.[10]

By 1959, the company was experiencing financial difficulties, and acquisition negotia-

Eagle Ottawa had almost as long a history as Albert Trostel & Sons. This picture outside the Grand Haven headquarters was taken in the 1920s.

tions were launched with Albert Trostel & Sons in Milwaukee. At the time, Trostel was the country's largest producer of side leather. On April 14, 1961, the *Grand Haven Daily Tribune* announced that the 96-year-old Eagle Ottawa would become a subsidiary of Trostel Industries Inc. in Milan, Tennessee. Everett Smith was named secretary of Eagle Ottawa at a board meeting held in May of that year.[11]

At the time of the merger, Albert O. Trostel Jr. said, "The only change we intend to accomplish is extensive expansion of the operations of this highly regarded company." According to the agreement, all current officers in the tannery were to continue under the new ownership, and Julian Hatton Jr. would continue as the president of Eagle Ottawa Leather Company. In all respects, the company would retain its corporate identity and management. Eagle Ottawa would continue to produce automobile, furniture, shoe, and mechanical leathers.[12]

Commenting on the sale, Hatton said, "I think it is a good thing for our firm and Grand Haven to become related to a much larger organization to give more strength to the operation." The announcement ended nervous speculation in Grand Haven about the future of one of the city's largest companies—one that employed 320 people there.[13]

For six years, Julian Hatton Jr. ran his company under the Trostel auspices. In 1967, he resigned to pursue other business interests. In 1969, Trostel executive Anders Segerdahl was named president.[14]

for more than a century—experienced some hard times throughout the decade.

By the mid-1960s, industrialized urban centers all over the Midwest were failing due to high labor costs, deteriorating neighborhoods, and expanded competition. So many cities were struggling that a string of Midwestern cities became known as the "Rust Belt," stretching from Minnesota to Detroit. Sadly, these financial problems were exacerbated in the leather industry by changing economics, tastes, and technologies. Domestic tanneries were fighting for their survival.

Although the 22-building Trostel tannery was known as one of the largest and most technologically advanced tanneries in Milwaukee, the company's overhead and production costs exceeded the amount of money it could make selling shoe leather in the current market.

"The total cost of upkeep was prohibitive," said treasurer Charles Krull, who joined Trostel in 1966. "That was just an economic fact of life. That facility, because of its age and location, was just not competitive in the international market."[15]

Furthermore, the company's product was rapidly becoming obsolete. So-called "hippies" and other members of the counterculture had embraced the moccasin as their shoe of choice, and the trend caught on. Subsequently, demand for Trostel's traditional, heavy-leather work shoe—a low-margin product to begin with—declined. Competition from South America continued to eat into profit margins. As if to flog a dying horse, market research suggested that any domestic tanning operations not in specialty leather production would suffer.[16]

Limited to side-leather production, the Milwaukee operation was hardly in the specialty-leather business. The tannery's outdated equipment did not allow for the kind of flexibility that was available

Inset: Scenes like this one inside Trostel's Milwaukee tannery during its heyday were increasingly rare by the 1960s, when the tannery was beset by economic problems brought on by competition.

Right: In 1969 the Albert Trostel board of directors voted to close the Milwaukee tannery. The building was boarded up and ultimately demolished.

EVERETT G. SMITH: A PROFILE

EVERETT SMITH, A CLOSE FRIEND AND partner of Albert O. Trostel Jr., was a Milwaukee native who rose from humble beginnings. Born on January 5, 1909, Smith's early years were filled with hardship due to the death of his father. Remarkably, his widowed mother, a woman of modest means, managed to send her son to the Milwaukee Country Day School and then to Dartmouth College, where Smith graduated in 1930. That same year, he joined Edgar Ricker & Company, a securities firm in Milwaukee, as a bond salesman.[1]

Smith was recruited to join Trostel in 1938 by Albert O. Trostel Jr.'s mother, Clara Uihlein Trostel, who recognized that Smith's financial credentials were well-suited to the company's needs.[2] Two years later, he was named treasurer. Eleven years later, he was elected executive vice president.[3]

Albert O. Trostel Jr. and Smith had been Dartmouth classmates; at the Trostel tannery, the two developed a close working relationship, and their skills complemented one another perfectly.

"Albert had more of an operations background, and the company was struggling a bit before Everett joined," said Tom Hauske Jr., Smith's grandson, who is one of the company's directors and corporate officers today. "Trostel realized that he needed additional financial expertise and business acumen in the organization. Everett Smith brought these characteristics to the business. As a result, they were successful partners for many years."[4]

Although the two men had an excellent working relationship, free of rancor and competition, history would favor the skills exhibited by Smith. Throughout the 1950s, the United States leather business peaked and then began to decline. Foreign competition was implacable, and the end was near for the great U.S. tanneries.

In 1962, when Trostel Jr. died, the company's board of directors named Smith to head Albert Trostel & Sons. He was charged with overseeing an expanding organization that included subsidiary firms in Wisconsin, three other states, and overseas. In many ways, however, this would only be the beginning of his contributions.

"Smith was a pretty quiet, behind-the-scenes guy," said Randy Perry, who is married to Smith's granddaughter, and would play an integral role in the company's success at the turn of the millennium as Trostel's president and chief operating officer. "Yet he was a very forceful and very powerful guy who pulled the company out—from a financial standpoint— and gave them the resources to continue to invest and grow the businesses."[5]

Smith's quiet yet forceful demeanor was fully evident during his years at the Trostel helm. Like many truly successful people Smith believed in the importance of ownership. Over the course of his life, he bought or started several companies, some of which fell under the Trostel umbrella. And like the Trostels before him, he decided to keep the company private, and, as the presence of Hauske Jr. and Perry indicate, he kept it in the family. Smith was careful not to micromanage.

"He didn't attempt to direct you, but he helped you wherever he could," said Frank Fermano, who worked for the company for nearly 50 years. "Everett Smith was just a prince of a guy."[6]

His support wasn't confined to the tannery or the office.

"Everett Smith was one of the greatest businessmen that I have had the pleasure of meeting and working with," said Charles Krull, who joined the company in 1966. "He was always concerned about people and their situation in life. There are many things that he did behind the scenes for individuals, and he did not seek any notoriety."

Smith was a well-rounded individual, which goes a long way toward explaining his long life. Throughout his 88 years, Smith was an active participant in the Milwaukee community. He served as trustee and director at Northwestern Mutual Life, and was a director at Badger Meter, Mattel Corp., Western Publishing, Jos. Schlitz Brewing Co., First Wisconsin, and the Milwaukee Blood Center. With his first wife, Gertrude Kasten, he had one daughter, Anita Smith Hauske.[7]

Smith was also an active sportsman. He played golf and sailed, and was, at one time, a Wisconsin state squash champion. Another one of Smith's major passions was baseball. After the Braves left Milwaukee for Atlanta in 1965, Smith joined six other investors, including Bud Selig—baseball's commissioner at this writing—in a quest to return professional baseball to Milwaukee.[8] In 1970, they purchased the American League's Seattle Pilots, promptly moved them to Milwaukee, and rechristened them the Brewers, in honor of Milwaukee's most famous industry.

Also known as a voracious reader, Smith kept an ongoing stack of trade journals and business literature, in addition to pleasure reading and Winston Churchill biographies.[9] He traveled widely and never missed the annual fall trade shows in Europe, visiting London and Paris.[10] Up until his death in 1997, it was not unusual to find Smith in the Trostel office five or six days a week.[11]

at the Eagle Ottawa plant, where workers had the capability to use the whole hide.[17]

Trostel's Milwaukee neighborhood had also become crime-ridden and dangerous. Employees' cars were vandalized, and it became difficult to find applicants for job vacancies. Trostel had to pay excessive amounts of overtime to maintain normal production levels. Lengthy discussions with local unions failed to produce satisfactory solutions for rising labor costs.[18]

During the fiscal years of 1968 and 1969, the Milwaukee and Milan leather operations lost a combined $1.7 million.[19] Taking all these factors into account, executives chose to cease operations in both Milwaukee and Milan at a board of directors meeting held May 23, 1969.[20]

"We came to the realization that the primary product that we historically had made was no longer viable in a U.S. manufacturing facility," said Krull. "Therefore, the decision was made to close the Milwaukee tannery in 1969. We laid off over 900 people."[21]

The factory was shut down. All the machinery and equipment was sold at auction. When it was determined that the buildings could not be sold, all but one was demolished. With leather no longer available from the Milwaukee plant, the Milan operation was sold to Genesco Inc. in 1970.[22]

"It was traumatic," Krull said. "It was quite a shock because we were the first in the Milwaukee area to close our operations. It was somewhat unexpected. It was basically viewed as something that could never happen because of the long history of the company."[23]

For Everett Smith, who had been named president only seven years earlier, the closing of the tannery was particularly hard to swallow. "It devastated Smith for maybe three or four years," recalled Albert O. Trostel III. "It was just a very, very difficult time in his life."[24]

For Trostel himself, the fourth generation of a family with leather in its blood, the decision—though not his to make—was "extremely difficult."[25] The fact that a father and his son—and then his son's son—had run the company was not unique to Trostel. Nor was it unusual for generations of the same working families to be laborers with the same company. "That generational thing was unique to the Milwaukee area, not only our tannery," said Krull. "Allis-Chalmers, all of the heavy manufacturers, were in a position where families would come to work for their entire careers. Furthermore, their children and their children's children were loyal workers for the same company. In that sense, [our closing] struck into the heart of families that were basically our workforce."[26]

Goodbye Shoes, Hello Cars

As hard as it was for emotional reasons, closing the Milwaukee tannery made perfect business sense. By the end of the 1960s, Trostel—especially through the Eagle Ottawa company—was catering to multiple industries in a vastly dif-

After he moved to Grand Haven in 1969, Anders Segerdahl refocused Eagle Ottawa on producing leather upholstery for the automobile business.

ferent competitive market than it had during its first century. Trostel boasted shoe leather, mechanical leather, and heavy leathers in its product arsenal. Now, with the addition of Eagle Ottawa, automotive and furniture upholstery leather provided the parent company with a good deal of versatility. And with versatility, opportunity would come.

A changing of the guard was also imminent. Hatton Jr., who had struggled to keep his own century-old family-run business on solid ground, decided to leave the firm in 1967 to pursue other interests. Two years later, as a decade of great change for Albert Trostel & Sons came to a close,

Anders Segerdahl was elected president of Eagle Ottawa and began to chart a new course.

Segerdahl's efforts to refocus Eagle Ottawa on the automobile industry would completely transform Trostel's leather-making capabilities over the next decade. In the coming years, the company would face more difficulties, but senior executives had developed a diversification strategy to weather market challenges. In addition to the growing operation at Eagle Ottawa, Trostel had the rubber and urethane-molding businesses at the Lake Geneva facility. Although the company's core business had been caught in the winds of global trade, the future looked promising.

The eighth painting in Albert Trostel's commemorative series is highly abstract and deeply symbolic, showing leather hanging limply on racks, waiting to be transformed into useful goods. Trostel underwent a series of changes after these paintings were created in the 1950s. By the 1990s, the company had become a significant manufacturer of plastic and rubber components as well.

CHAPTER EIGHT

FOCUS, FOCUS, FOCUS!

1970–1989

Bob Gamache would tell me, "Karch, go get the order. Figure out how to make it later."

—Merrill Karcher

AS THE 1960s DREW TO A CLOSE, Albert Trostel & Sons had more than 110 years worth of endeavors included in its organizational chart. There were Trostel Compounding Ltd. and Trostel Tool and Die, both in Wisconsin. Two other companies, Trostel Industries Inc., and Trostel Mechanical Industries Inc., had been formed in Milan, Tennessee, but absorbed back into the Lake Geneva operation.

Trostel Aviation Co. Inc. still provided aircraft for transportation between company sites. The planes, when not in use, were leased to other companies. Trostel Trading Co. was organized to export cattle hair and leather scraps. Finally, Midwest Oil & Protein Co. transformed tanning wastes into oil and protein.[1]

The largest of these companies was Albert Trostel Packings Ltd., which operated from Lake Geneva, producing industrial leather and compression-molded rubber parts for Bendix and Whirlpool Corp.

In 1971, after Everett Smith and Anders Segerdahl had acquired a percentage ownership in Albert Trostel & Sons, Smith set up Everett Smith Investments to consolidate his ownership in Trostel and other businesses.[2]

Despite his partial ownership, Smith never became directly involved in Eagle Ottawa, but he trusted fellow Trostel veteran Anders Segerdahl to manage that side of the business. In the coming decade, under the leadership of Segerdahl, Eagle Ottawa would steadily assume greater importance in Albert Trostel & Sons' history.

Segerdahl Goes to Eagle Ottawa

When he arrived in Grand Haven, Michigan, Anders Segerdahl found a company still in need of overhaul. In the first seven years after Trostel bought the company, Eagle Ottawa did not once turn a profit. But at the end of 1969, Segerdahl's first year with Eagle Ottawa, the company was $15,000 in the black.[3]

Despite the modest profit, Segerdahl recognized several problems—a lack of focus combined with the same difficulties that had plagued Albert Trostel and other tanneries. Eagle Ottawa couldn't compete against foreign manufacturers of shoe-leather products, yet it fared well in regard to at least one product line—automobile upholstery.

Over the next few years, Segerdahl turned Eagle Ottawa's attention to this one market segment. He first pulled the company out of its unprofitable product lines, including furniture and footwear.

Eagle Ottawa, purchased by Albert Trostel in 1961, was headquartered in Grand Haven, Michigan. The tanner had a diverse operation, with a major stake in automobile seats.

Above: Charles Krull, who was Albert Trostel & Sons vice president of finance, was credited by Trostel Packings' Bob Gamache for his investment in technology.

Below: Under Anders Segerdahl, Eagle Ottawa spent the 1970s and 1980s focusing more intently on car seats, eventually winning business from each of the Big Three automakers.

The 1970s saw two major oil crises, however—the first in 1973 and the second in 1979—and demand for fuel-efficient vehicles soared during the decade. The Big Three—which had long met the demand for roomy gas guzzlers like GM's Cadillac and speedy muscle cars like Ford's Mustang—would respond with economy cars like the Chevrolet Chevette.

"We were negatively affected during those two time periods," said Charles Krull. "Our customers were not producing the same amount or the types of automobiles that they had in the past."[4]

For their part, the Japanese diligently pursued the American market, and they approached manufacturing in a completely new way, applying new concepts to the assembly line. In the process, they reduced their manufacturing costs, labor costs, and development time between new models. Toyota and Honda also designed engines that were more fuel-efficient and lighter than those found under the hoods of American cars.

While the Japanese automakers slowly penetrated the American market, their low-end cars were rarely outfitted in leather. In Europe, companies like Mercedes-Benz and Volvo relied on long-time suppliers. Segerdahl managed to land a small contract with the Swedish company, but he quickly realized that Eagle Ottawa needed to land a major contract with at least one of the Big Three.

We were down to 7.5 percent of the total automotive leather in the United States. We were the low one on the totem. I said, "How in the hell are you going to sell here?" So, for various

Eagle Ottawa and the Automobile Industry

Although Segerdahl had Eagle Ottawa focused on automotive upholstery, he and the company faced an uphill battle. The 1970s was an extremely trying decade for the American automobile industry. Imports from England and Germany enjoyed a niche in the U.S. market, but they tended to be pricier than domestic cars manufactured by the Big Three—Chrysler, Ford, and General Motors. Soon, however, upstarts from Japan—namely, Toyota and Honda—began importing their cheap, fuel-efficient compact cars to America. Derided as low-quality knock-offs, no one in the industry considered them much of a threat—at first.

Next, he removed Eagle Ottawa from businesses that were making money—including men's belts, dog collars, and leashes—but had little volume.

reasons, I had the best chance with Ford Motor Company because our competitor had an "in" with General Motors ... I worked very hard with our salespeople.[5]

The effort paid off. By the end of the 1970s, Eagle Ottawa had become one of the largest suppliers of Ford upholstery leather. Segerdahl next approached Chrysler with a specialty called "Corinthian leather." Chrysler liked what it saw and soon was conducting business with Eagle Ottawa. There were some difficult moments, Segerdahl remembered, when Chrysler had financial difficulties, but calamity was avoided.

"That was a scary situation," said Segerdahl. "When the *Wall Street Journal* one morning had them in bankruptcy, we had our total working capital in receivables."[6]

From that point on, any problems Eagle Ottawa experienced with the car industry were unrelated to product. Chrysler's continuing financial difficulties spurred Eagle Ottawa to put a $250,000 cap on the account, a move that annoyed Chrysler's executives. Eventually the automaker refused the deal and the supplier agreement was terminated with hard feelings on both sides. It took 15 years for Eagle Ottawa to regain Chrysler's business.

Meanwhile, Segerdahl approached General Motors, again with a new product. This one was called Nudo, the Spanish word for "naked." "That really woke them up," said Segerdahl. "Their styling department and their purchasing department came to Grand Haven to take a look at what we had done."[7]

GM was impressed—both with the product and Eagle Ottawa's Grand Haven facility—but the automaker was not about to sign on unconditionally. General Motors' purchasing executives awarded a six-month contract to Eagle Ottawa, predicting that another competitor would knock off Nudo at a discount. GM was frank about its doubt that Eagle Ottawa could maintain such a high-quality product for long. Fortunately, General Motors was wrong.

During the 1970s Segerdahl steadily built Eagle Ottawa's market share of American automotive leather. It would fluctuate between 15 percent and 20 percent, but Segerdahl and Eagle Ottawa had made their mark.

Anders Segerdahl, who started with Albert Trostel & Sons as an apprentice in 1948, took over the Eagle Ottawa helm in 1969. By the end of the 1980s, his vision helped create a full-service automotive leather supplier with international scope.

By the end of the decade, Eagle Ottawa had phased out all leather production not associated with the automobile industry.[8] "I will never forget the day when we were running 12,000 hides a week for automotive," said Segerdahl. "That was a big day for us."[9]

But Eagle Ottawa remained a tanner first and foremost. It was a major leather supplier for the North American automobile industry and had even become the first American tannery to penetrate the Japanese automotive market. Eagle's first contracts in Japan, which had a relatively small market for hides, were with Toyota and Honda in 1978. Yet the fundamental changes in the industry presented both a challenge and an

ANDERS SEGERDAHL: A PROFILE

ANDERS SEGERDAHL WAS BORN IN Sweden in 1923.[1] Like Albert O. Trostel Jr., Segerdahl was born into a tanning business that had been part of his family for generations. During World War II, when many European tannery workers were drafted, Anders' grandfather told him it was time to go to work during summers. "Instead of pursuing something else, my grandfather said, 'Now you start working in the tannery,' but I never liked the tanning," explained Segerdahl. "I had the pleasure to sit at Sunday dinners during the Depression and listen to those terrible stories about all our customers that couldn't pay their bills."[2] Those conversations gave the 10-year-old boy a very negative impression of the family business.[3]

While Segerdahl agreed to work in the tannery during his summer vacations, he was determined to pave his own path. "I changed my schoolwork a little bit to be more business-oriented than engineering-oriented, as I wanted to do from the beginning," Segerdahl explained.[4] In 1944 he graduated from Pahlmans School of Economics in Stockholm with a degree in finance and business administration.[5] A year later, while attending officer's school, he received the requisite permission from the King of Sweden to leave the country. Despite his early resistance to the family business, Segerdahl left for Argentina to learn the tanning business.

> My family had done business with an old firm in Buenos Aires called ECA Otero HNOS, and it was time for one of our family members to go down and meet with those people. At one particular time, we did not only buy hides from Argentina; we also bought a tanning material called quebracho. And we had our own factory to make tanning material, [to] leech the tanning acid out of that wood.[6]

Segerdahl established himself in Argentina and became familiar with the tanning process and products. "Quebracho means breaking the axe," according to Segerdahl. "It is the hardest wood in the world. It doesn't even float in water. It sinks."[7] Segerdahl spent about two years with the Buenos Aires firm. "The idea at the beginning was to take some of the family's money and to build a tannery in Argentina to support our own tanneries," he said. However, with the unstable Argentine economy, that proposal was eventually scrapped and Segerdahl moved on, leaving behind any thoughts of building a tannery and instead seeking to learn new tanning methods.[8]

Following his instincts, Segerdahl moved to the cutting edge of the industry. He was aware that during World War II, American tanneries had revolutionized their methods to meet the needs of the military. So he moved to the United States to learn what he could. "I was extremely lucky to become an apprentice at Albert Trostel & Sons in 1948," he recalled.[9] Grateful for the opportunity, Segerdahl thrived in his new position. "The Trostel family was extremely encouraging to me and helpful. So was the Everett Smith family."[10]

One of Segerdahl's early proponents was none other than Clara Uihlein Trostel. When the 25-year-old Swede first visited Milwaukee in 1948, Clara liked to invite him to have tea with her on Saturdays. Segerdahl was proficient in many languages and charmed Clara by speaking German with her. Clara always insisted that half their conversation be in English so Segerdahl would learn this country's language as well.

Segerdahl found a good fit in Milwaukee. "Mr. Trostel asked if I wouldn't like to stay on," he said, discussing the end of his apprenticeship.[11] Segerdahl explained to Trostel that he and his fiancée, Birgit, a fellow Swede who was in Milwaukee attending Downer College, had plans to return home to be married. "I [did] have an obligation to my family," Segerdahl said. "I [was] the oldest grandson. I [had] new ideas how to run a tanning company in Sweden."[12] Trostel had difficulty understanding why Segerdahl would leave after doing so well in the industry and becoming close friends with the Milwaukee tannery families. As Segerdahl was leaving for Europe, Trostel remarked, "I bet you that you will come back."[13]

Segerdahl and Birgit returned to Sweden where they were married and started a family. Drawing from his knowledge of global markets and emerging tannery technology, Segerdahl believed that his old family business would thrive only if more of its profits could be reinvested in operations, as it was done at Trostel. "I tried very hard to buy out some of my relatives who had ownership in the tanneries," said Segerdahl.[14] But the business had been in the family for 200 years, and many of Segerdahl's relatives had become highly dependent on the dividends. Naturally, they were resistant.

"They said no, and I got a little provoked," Segerdahl acknowledged. He quickly became convinced that he would be unable to manage the situation successfully. Resignedly, Segerdahl told his family, "You know, my hands are tied."[15]

"At that time, the Trostel family found out about this and asked if I would like to come back and work," Segerdahl said. "It took only about thirty minutes—less than that, three minutes—for my wife and me to make up our minds and go back to the United States."[16]

The decision was easy, but transition was initially difficult. "We started out from scratch," Segerdahl said.[17] He went from manning the corporate offices to toiling on the plant floor, from being the executive head of a family business to donning overalls and heavy shoes and working with chromium—albeit in a supervisory capacity. "Well, I looked at myself," he said, "and well, that's a start at the beginning, as we say."[18] Segerdahl, though, was motivated and liked the challenge. "Let's see what's going to happen," he declared. In no time, his talents were recognized and rewarded. "It didn't take very long until they asked if I would like to take over the hide buying at Trostel. In those days, we were using approximately 32,000 hides a week."[19]

Hide buying brought Segerdahl into the inner circle of management.

I reported, in those days, every week to Mr. Smith because he previously did the hide buying. I also consulted with Mr. Trostel on a daily basis. On Saturdays, we had lunch together and we went over the sales and the purchases to see if we were in balance. That was how we discussed our performance and how much we shipped out and sold.[20]

Hide buying was a complex matter. The company was buying hides from many dealers and was hedging some of its purchases on the hide exchange. Segerdahl, juggling a direct line to the hide exchange and any number of hide dealers, was a busy man.

He likes to tell about an Englishman who came into his office one day when Segerdahl was on the phone. The visitor remarked, "I never heard of a person being able to do deals, talk to a dozen people, at the same time." Segerdahl said he would typically be talking on two or three telephones and smoking two cigarettes.[21]

From his position as hide buyer, Segerdahl moved to sales and purchasing. In the late 1950s and early 1960s, the tannery was producing leather primarily for boots and shoes. Of the 32,000 weekly hides, 98 percent were used for shoes and boots. The Trostel tannery enjoyed an excellent reputation among customers in the work-shoe business.[22]

In those days we had a glorious thing. First of all, we had a big market in the cowboy-boot business. We had a big market in the work-shoe business. The medium- to the low-priced women's shoes were a big market for us also. Some of our big customers were Genesco, Brown Shoe Company, B. B. Walker, Texas Boot, International Shoe, H. H. Brown, and Weinbrenner.[23]

In 1969, Segerdahl started his second career with the company. Elected president of Eagle Ottawa—a position he would hold for 30 years—Segerdahl began to chart a new course for the parent company.

opportunity for Eagle Ottawa. It could complete its transformation into a full-service automotive supplier—one that designed and sewed, in addition to providing leather—or it could risk being swept aside in a fiercely competitive global market.

Packings Struggles

As with Eagle Ottawa's move toward automotive leather, Trostel Packings' transition from a producer of mechanical leather to one that also manufactured rubber molded parts and synthetics was gradual and organic, as the subsidiary worked to meet the demands of a changing marketplace. Still, the early 1970s was a difficult time for Albert Trostel Packings Ltd. After distributing profits to the struggling tannery for years, reinvestment capital began to come the subsidiary's way when the parent company closed the tannery in 1969. But the neglect had caught up with Trostel Packings, and it began to fade into the red.

"Just about the full time I was there, we were losing money," said Albert Trostel III, who, for a few years in the early 1970s, was president of the subsidiary, while Frank Fermano served as vice president. "I finally decided that if I was a boss, I'd fire me. So I left."[10] He would stay on the board of directors, but Albert O. Trostel III's departure in 1973 marked the end of an era for the company. Everett Smith had been running the company for 11 years, but for the first time since its inception 115 years earlier, Albert Trostel & Sons did not employ a Trostel.

Frank Fermano, who at this point had been with the company in some capacity or another for 37 years, resumed his presidency and was set to enter his third decade with Albert Trostel Packings Ltd. Fermano was regarded as a classic Trostel executive—involved, available, and fair. "He was a great person to work for," said his assistant, Nancy Schlicher, who joined Trostel Packings in 1968. "He would go out in the plant every day, and he always had a policy that his door was open. Anyone who needed to talk to him, all they had to do was call and he was always available."[11]

Joyce Huck, who joined the subsidiary's sales department in 1971, witnessed much more than presidencies changing hands in her 31 years with the company. For starters, computers were not used, and the sales department, like so many others at the time, was a decidedly low-tech operation.

Every time we got an order, it was divided into certain shipments—like 100 pieces every week for a month or so. We'd have an aperture card for each one of those shipments. We called them commitment cards. After we'd make our shipments, we would have to divest them from those cards, and they would go into a department. We had what we called a tub. It looked like a little Ferris wheel that rotated around with rows and

Frank Fermano (left) joined Trostel in 1936, moved to Trostel Packings upon its inception in 1952, and stayed with the company until 1985. George Corsi, a sales manager with Trostel rival Federal Mogul, is pictured at right.

Bob Gamache joined Trostel Packings as an engineer in 1976. He would later head the Albert Trostel & Sons subsidiary when Frank Fermano retired in 1985.

rows of cards for shipments. Everything was done by hand.[12]

Eventually, the sales process would become much more streamlined when computers replaced cards and wheels. The culture, Huck said, would also change as Trostel Packings' products grew more precise.

When I first started, we were a real close-knit group. We didn't make precision parts, so it wasn't so tense. They were good quality, but not precision. Through the years, as we built the business up, it became all automotive. You had to make sure everything was precision. We hired more quality people.[13]

One of those people was Bob Gamache, a young methods engineer. In 1976, while working

for the International Packing Corporation, one of Trostel's rivals, Gamache learned from a head-hunter that Trostel was looking for someone with molding technology experience. "I had the molding knowledge, the tool and dye knowledge, the methods engineering knowledge," said Gamache. "So it was an excellent fit for me and for Trostel."[14]

Gamache, like Segerdahl with Eagle Ottawa, joined an Albert Trostel & Sons subsidiary that was doing many things right but lacked focus.

We had our toes in many, many things, but we didn't have our feet in any of them. We had a muffler factory. We were in the aftermarket, but we did not have a complete list of items to be in the aftermarket. We were in the oil seal business, but we didn't have any rubber seals; all we had was leather seals.[15]

To garner interest in Trostel Packings' products, Gamache began to give away samples. "We used to joke and say, 'I can't believe he gives all these parts away,' " said Huck. "And he used to say, 'Well, you have to give it away to get the business.' "[16]

Gamache, it turned out, was right on the money. "We started getting all this business, and we just kept growing so fast," said Huck. "The first time we shipped $1 million in one month, we had a big party in the cafeteria."[17]

Like Albert O. Trostel Jr. in the decades before him, Gamache saw that an investment in technology was the key to future success. Fortunately, he had an ally in Chuck Krull. "Chuck had the clairvoyance that this thing should go forward," Gamache said. "He was of tremendous assistance to me on the financial side. He really believed in technology—that we could spend a little bit of money."[18]

With Krull's approval, an injection-molding machine was purchased, and Gamache was placed in charge of the engineering department under Fermano, who was still heading the subsidiary. At this point, Trostel Packings began to specialize in custom seals and precision molding, with which Gamache was well-acquainted dating back to his International Packing days. With Merrill Karcher, who Gamache described as a "very fine innovator,"[19] Trostel Packings, like Eagle Ottawa, began to consolidate.

EAGLE OTTAWA PROCESS

DEVELOPING AND MAINTAINING A HOLD on the automotive leather market was no easy matter. "We are the guys who take a stinky raw hide [and convert it to] the seasoned leather that people sit on," joked Helmut Beutel, who has been with Eagle Ottawa since 1990. "It takes a lot of patience and a lot of trial and error."[1]

Patience is something Beutel understands well. He began his tanning education in Germany in the 1950s, and worked for chemical giant BASF before joining Eagle Ottawa's research and development team. By 2003, Beutel was vice president of the company's global research and development.[2]

The biggest challenge to making automotive leather is meeting carmakers' exacting standards. The first step is choosing the hides well. "You can only use some types of animals," Beutel said.[3] Different cow breeds produce different quality hides, depending on their age, eating habits, and living environment.

And much like humans, as animals age, their skin fibers become stretched, so it's important to purchase hides from younger animals whose skin is still supple. Further, the best leather comes from the heavy, native steers that are grown for meat. Eagle Ottawa buys steers from the United States, especially from the northern part of the country—Montana and Nebraska—where the colder climate produces better hides. The company also buys some hides from Argentina, Europe, and South Africa to support those regional operations.[4]

Once the hides reach the plant, they must be prepared for tanning, an important step that also involves the input of the research and development team. Beutel explained how they might be involved in the process of removing hair.

Each and every animal changes like we do in every season. A winter hide has about six or seven pounds more hair on it. You have to approach that hide differently to remove the hair. That process can actually destroy a hide if you are not very careful with your chemicals. You have to remove the hair without damaging the hide. You have to remove the flesh without damaging it.[5]

The salt of burned metals, especially chromium, tans hides very quickly and very economically. The salt of chrome is also the easiest to use and the most valuable because of the benefits it supplies to the leather. Beutel noted that it doesn't decay or shrink in boiling water. The tanning process itself takes about 16 hours; from start to finish it takes about four weeks for a salted hide to become a car seat.[6]

Research and development is continually involved in the selection of chemicals—a tricky situation because of the sheer number available. In the whole process, Eagle Ottawa uses 100 to 210 different chemicals. About 1,000 are used for tanning, but only about a fifth or a sixth of those are used for automotive leather tanning.

Coloring hides for the auto industry is another chemically complex process, one that Eagle takes seriously. Every year, auto manufacturers introduce new colors, requiring Eagle Ottawa to develop matching interior colors for leather. "It can take four or five weeks to do that," said Beutel. "There are dyestuffs available by the thousands."[7]

Eagle Ottawa meets customers' design needs by employing four designers—one in Germany, one in Italy, and two in the United States, including Pat Oldenkamp, Eagle's vice president of global design, who is based in Rochester Hills, Michigan.

"Our design representatives are members of industry associations such as the Color Marketing Group, the Detroit Color Council, the United States Color Association, and the Japan Fashion Color Association," said Oldenkamp, who joined Eagle Ottawa in 1993 from Ford Motor Company. These affiliations, Oldenkamp added, lend the company "a lot of credibility in the industry."[8]

By 2003, Eagle Ottawa's research and development effort had paid off impressively. The company boasted a library with information on more than 1,000 tested dyes.[9]

Eagle in the Driver's Seat

Eagle Ottawa entered the 1980s in much better shape than it had entered the previous decade. With 10 years under his belt as president, Anders Segerdahl had cut the fat from the company's product line, focusing on Detroit's Big Three automakers.

Although the Big Three had responded to the Japanese competition during the oil crises of the 1970s, Chrysler, Ford, and GM had their own internal problems, which would open the door further for the Japanese companies. Chrysler, Ford, and GM were bound by tradition, restrictive unions, top-heavy management, and outmoded factories.

Gradually, as the Japanese cars improved in quality, many American consumers shed their loyalty to American companies and bought Japanese cars by the thousands. The Big Three had been outfoxed, and they began to study and adopt Japanese manufacturing techniques while going through wrenching waves of downsizing. Tens of thousands of factory workers lost their jobs as plants were moved overseas, and thousands of white-collar employees were laid off.

Despite the instability in Detroit and Chrysler's lingering bad feelings, Eagle Ottawa soldiered on, solidifying its production for Ford and GM throughout the 1980s, and establishing business with the Japanese car manufacturers. With some American assembly-line work heading overseas, coupled with the success of the Japanese car manufacturers, Segerdahl and Eagle Ottawa began to think globally. But first they acted locally. By the time Chrysler allowed Eagle Ottawa back into the fold, the tanner had outgrown its Grand Haven facility.[20] A Chicago-based company helped Eagle Ottawa find a site for a new tannery in Waterloo, Iowa. According to Jim Orth, who has worked in finance for the parent company since 1984, the location made perfect strategic sense because of its close proximity to a large meat packing plant that would go on to become a major supplier of hides for Eagle.

[The new tannery site] was carefully planned. We looked at where the source of hides was, and was moving to, rather than where the customers or the product would be. Locating a tannery close to the source of hides reduces the cost of getting those hides into the tannery and also gives you good access.[21]

By the 1980s, Eagle Ottawa boasted a state-of-the-art tanning process. Wet hides were trimmed and sorted before a series of chemical baths removed hair and excess flesh. Hides were then "bated" (to remove alkalinity) and "pickled" (to increase acidity). Only after all these steps were completed did the hides undergo tanning, which stabilized the material, protecting it from rotting and putrefaction.

Product and Geographic Expansion

Eagle Tanning Company, as the subsidiary was known, launched in Waterloo in 1988. Around that time, Eagle Ottawa began bypassing brokers and buying hides directly from packing houses at regulated prices. The new facility and the change in purchasing were significant, but Segerdahl was far from finished with transforming the company.

The Bermans, a family of Polish immigrants who had come to Detroit to escape Nazi persecution during World War II, had been freelance cutting for Eagle Ottawa since 1951. They were now cutting leather for automotive seating for Chrysler and GM, two of Eagle's customers. "Why don't you let us cut leather to specification?" Segerdahl asked his auto industry customers. "'You don't have to have any inventory. You know how many Cadillacs and Pontiacs you need in a certain day, and we can ship those sets to you.' They bought that."[23]

Next, Segerdahl had to sell his proposition to the Bermans. He offered the family a $12 million buyout. According to Segerdahl, they scoffed at the price,[24] but soon a five-year profit-sharing deal was struck with the Berman family. After the five years, Eagle Ottawa assumed ownership of the Bermans' facility.

Now one step closer to becoming a full-service automotive upholstery supplier, Eagle Ottawa's next major step was to go international. It happened rather serendipitously, recalled Segerdahl. Eagle Ottawa had been purchasing pretanned hides from Pierpoint & Bryant, a Warrington, England-based company which had a capacity of 3,000 hides per week.[25]

I went over to take a look at [the tannery], and I couldn't believe my eyes. People were standing out in the rain and the snow, tanning and doing all kinds of work. Windowpanes and part of the roof were missing.[26]

As the first tannery built in the United States in "a long, long time," the Waterloo facility had other advantages, according to Orth. Many of the older tanneries, he explained, suffered from poor layout. At Waterloo, product did not have to be moved from one floor to the next. "It had one floor and state-of-the-art equipment, including computerized process-monitoring," Orth noted. "It advanced our manufacturing capabilities and resulted in significant cost savings."[22]

Segerdahl would soon have a chance to restore the struggling tannery. Vacationing in Florida, he received a call from a Pierpoint & Bryant representative who told Segerdahl that the British tannery was on the verge of bankruptcy. An auction was set for the next day.[27] Everett Smith was also in Florida, but Segerdahl couldn't reach him, so Eagle's president made an arrangement with Charles Krull, Trostel's vice president of finance.[28] Segerdahl remembered the next day's conversation with Smith:

Segerdahl: "I just bought the tannery."
Smith: "Good for you. Where did you buy it?"
Segerdahl: "I bought it in Warrington."
Smith: "Oh, that's great. How much did you pay for it?"
Segerdahl: "Well, £750,000."
Smith: "All right, we will make arrangements. I will tell the board of directors this was an emergency."[29]

A coup was more like it. "We built it up to 12,000 to 14,000 hides per week without borrowing too much money," said Segerdahl. "It's now a very modern tannery, and it's very important for our European market."[30]

With Eagle Ottawa's initial dip into international waters, Segerdahl now had Albert Trostel & Sons' automotive leather subsidiary poised for a major breakthrough. His spur-of-the-moment acquisition could not have been made if Albert Trostel & Sons had not remained privately held through the years. Once again, the company's reinvestment strategy paved the way for future victories. If the 1980s was eventful for Eagle Ottawa, the coming decade would be best described as a whirlwind.

Packings Phases Out Leather

Throughout more than 100 years of business, Albert Trostel & Sons proved that it could change with the marketplace. Anders Segerdahl and Everett Smith understood what their customers wanted. Customer service was crucial, so they began setting up shop closer to the carmakers. Full service was important, so they added value.

Albert Trostel Packings Ltd. had also changed with the marketplace. By the early 1980s, companies such as Monsanto and DuPont began to "fill in the gray area," as Bob Gamache put it,[31] between rubber and urethane. The resulting products, which were processed similarly to rubber, went under a number of names, including TPR, thermoplastic rubber, TPU, thermoplastic urethane, and

rigid thermoplastics. Trostel saw potential in the work and began developing its own product. Before long, Trostel Packings signed a contract with Briggs & Stratton to supply seals. The modern products were created from TPUs and had the sealing capabilities of rubber along with the wear characteristics of urethane.[32]

By the mid-1980s, the subsidiary's transformation from a producer of mechanical leather to a manufacturer of molded rubber and plastics was complete.

"In 1952 we were probably producing 90 percent leather products and only 10 percent rubber products," recalled Trostel Packings President Frank Fermano, who had been there the whole time. "This thing reversed itself over the years, and in 1985, we finally sold off the leather operation and just manufactured molded rubber and plastics."[33]

In 1985, Fermano retired after a remarkable 49 years with the company. "Frank was an excellent person," said Bob Gamache. "He was really the founder, the person who believed in this company, and brought it forward into Lake Geneva in 1952."[34]

Gamache took over for the departed Fermano. As head of Trostel Packings' engineering department, Gamache pushed for focus and product development; during his presidency, these two ingredients became Trostel Packings' mantra. "Innovation. Protect your customer. Protect your flank," Gamache said. "Just be the very best at three or four things instead of trying to be all things and competing with everyone."[35]

Customization would play an integral role in Gamache's strategy. "When Bob Gamache took over as president, he decided we had to go custom and get rid of a lot of our small customers," said Joyce Huck. "At the time, we had a $25 minimum order, which was nothing, and we changed it to $1,000, which eliminated all these little companies that would buy just a handful of parts."[36]

Whereas competitors were, as Karcher put it, "catalogue-oriented," Trostel Packings catered more personally to its customers.[37] As if to underscore this dedication to customer service and new products, two new facilities opened in 1985. The subsidiary's Polyurethane Division relocated its production facility to a new 19,000-square-foot building in Lake Geneva and entered the injection-molding industry. To house Merrill Karcher's customer-driven innovations, Trostel Packings opened a research and development center in Lake Geneva.

"What do you want? We'll design it for you," Karcher remembered the sales staff saying to customers. "Bob Gamache would tell me, 'Karch, go get the order. Figure out how to make it later.'" At least one of the products that Karcher "figured out" was a major success. Using a DuPont polymer, Karcher developed a wheel-bearing seal with performance superior to others on the market. It withstood the friction of a wheel bearing and thus boasted a longer life. It also held up to the cold North American climes better than previous wheel-bearing seals. These seals, which were made from a DuPont compound known as Vamac, extended the lives of wheel bearings from about 24,000 miles of use to about 150,000 miles.[38]

By 1987, Trostel Packings launched production of Vamac from a 4,000-square-foot facility in Lake Geneva. "We were immediately in need of additional space," recalled Tim Baker, who was hired by the subsidiary four years earlier as an accountant.[39] The Albert Trostel & Sons subsidiary began scouting for new territory, and after a national search, ended up selecting Whitewater,

Above: Merrill Karcher, Trostel Packings' resident innovator, teamed with Bob Gamache to develop a more customer-friendly product line.

Below: The Trostel Packings plant, pictured in 1986.

Wisconsin, for a new plant. Baker said he looked at a number of criteria.

We wanted to be near our customers, near our suppliers, and be near our existing facility for technical support and component support. We looked in a number of places, and in the end we built a matrix and placed a value on each specific criterion. [We] decided that the location needed to be near our technical support, which was in Lake Geneva. We got a number of inducements by the city of Whitewater and the state of Wisconsin to locate there.[40]

Whitewater was a small town of only about 10,000, with many of the residents connected to the University of Wisconsin. The town had a very small industrial base. There was, however, a fairly new industrial park available. It took Trostel Packings about 18 months to build its new 40,000-square-foot greenfield manufacturing plant.

"It was a make-or-buy decision, and ownership had enough clairvoyance to see that if we invested, we'd get our money back," said Gamache.[41]

In the meantime, 29 miles away in Lake Geneva, business was quite good for Trostel Packings' Polyurethane Division. By 1989, four years after its opening, the facility had expanded by 39,000 feet to house lab, testing, and new production capabilities. For Albert Trostel Packings Ltd., the gray area between rubber and urethane would soon cease to exist, enabling Gamache and his team to narrow their focus even more.

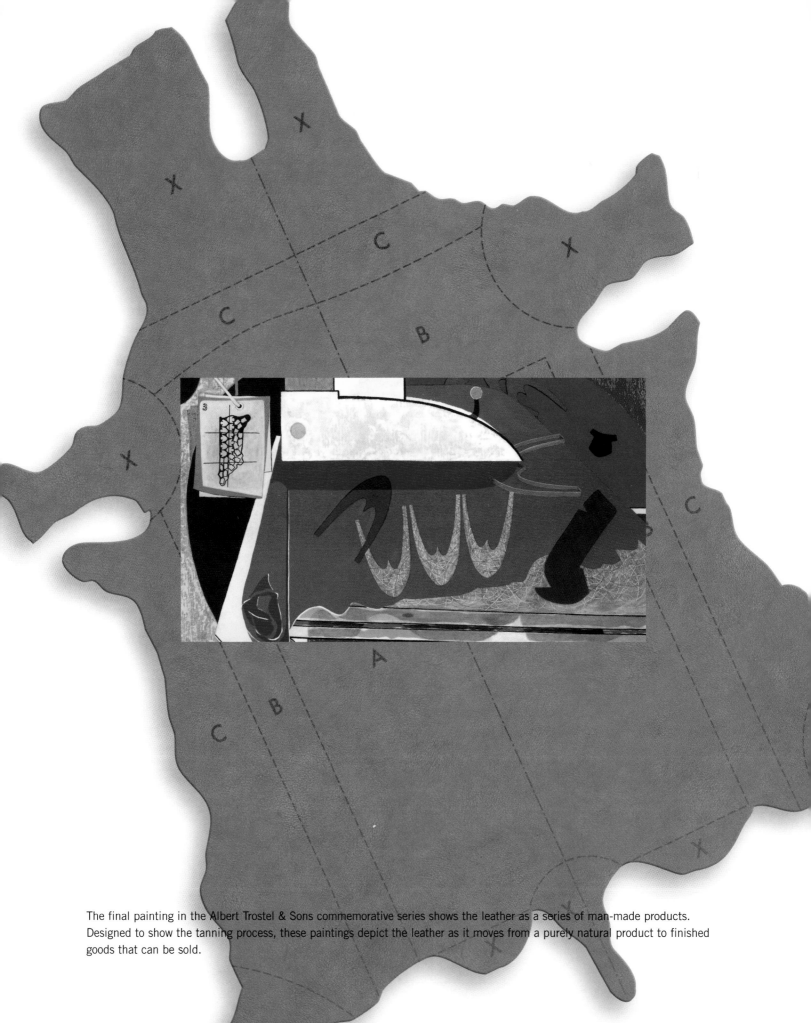

The final painting in the Albert Trostel & Sons commemorative series shows the leather as a series of man-made products. Designed to show the tanning process, these paintings depict the leather as it moves from a purely natural product to finished goods that can be sold.

CHAPTER NINE

NEW LEADERSHIP IN A DECADE OF GLOBALIZATION

1990–1999

Everett Smith's long-term perspective on business provided stability for the company. His longevity and passion for business were key factors in leading the organization through rapid growth and setting the stage for lasting success.

—Tom Hauske Jr.,
on his grandfather's legacy

ALBERT TROSTEL & SONS HAD always been a family business, but with Albert O. Trostel III's departure—first from the Trostel Packings subsidiary in 1973 and then from the board of directors a decade later—the parent company lost its last Trostel.

Everett Smith—who was now the majority shareholder in all the Trostel companies, under his Everett Smith Investments holding company—made it a family company again in 1992, when he and Anders Segerdahl asked Randy Perry to join Albert Trostel Packings. Perry, whose mother-in-law was Smith's only child, had been working in corporate finance and living with his wife in Manhattan, but the couple was open to new possibilities.

"We were weighing our options about where we wanted to go as a family," Perry recalled. "We didn't have any children at the time, but we weren't all that excited about raising a family in New York City. It was a good time for a transition."[1]

Perry met with Segerdahl in Milwaukee, to discuss a sales and marketing role for Perry at Trostel Packings, which was looking to grow the urethane and thermoplastic side of the business. Perry had a marketing background, and his interest was piqued.[2]

"It was a good fit, very new to me," Perry said. "Manufacturing is very different from what I was doing in finance and banking, but I was excited about the challenge and took it on."[3]

Still, his job wouldn't be easy. The Polyurethane Division's sales to the tire and wheel market for electric forklifts had reached maturity. "The challenge there," Perry said, "was to get the last big customer in order to get a dominant position and become the clear number one in the tire and wheel market."[4]

In seeking market dominance for the Polyurethane Division business, Perry's challenges would prove far more difficult than a mature market.

"The thermoplastic segment of the Polyurethane Division was very small and didn't have a lot of structure to it, and it didn't have a good sales and marketing strategy," Perry said. "We got into it by accident. Customers who knew us from rubber molding and urethane molding said, 'By the way, can you do this?'[5] Despite the lack of planning, Perry saw the possibilities.

We had less than $1 million in sales, but we saw an opportunity to serve a regional customer

The Trostel logo conveyed a different message in 1990 than in 1952. By that time, Trostel Packings had transitioned into urethane, thermoplastics, and rubber products.

base in thermoplastics in the automotive, appliance and hand-tool market, where we had done work on the rubber side.[6]

Although he was an industry newcomer, Perry had clearly learned a great deal in a short period of time from Anders Segerdahl. Keenly aware of how the business had evolved—from leather seals to synthetic seals to urethane seals, and finally to thermoplastic seals—Perry set forth to change what he described as "reactive selling" practices.[7]

Eagle Cuts, Sews, and Designs

Anders Segerdahl was determined to maintain Eagle Ottawa's momentum as the 1980s gave way to the 1990s. His was hardly an easy task. By the beginning of the decade, the car industry had transformed into an entirely different beast than when Albert Trostel & Sons purchased Eagle in 1961. Companies like Ford and GM were outsourcing much of their production, looking to suppliers to provide complete component systems, rather than parts.

At the same time, the lines had blurred between foreign and domestic manufacturers in this truly global industry. Japanese companies had built huge assembly plants throughout the U.S., and domestic manufacturers had established plants all over the globe. Suppliers shipped parts worldwide to factories that in turn shipped completed cars globally.

In its bid to become a full-service automotive leather supplier, Eagle Ottawa aimed to add cutting to its repertoire. Now that the financial agreement with the Berman family had elapsed, Eagle Ottawa assumed ownership of the Bermans' Rochester Hills, Michigan, Mastercraft Leather facility. The cutting business was faring well for Eagle, but Segerdahl not only wanted to cut leather, he also wanted to cut costs.

We had moved three times to bigger and better facilities. The last one that we bought from the Bermans was about 125,000 square feet. Then we started to look at where we could cut less expensively than in Rochester Hills. We started to investigate Mexico, and we found that we ought to move to Juarez because we had some customers in that area.[8]

Perhaps Segerdahl was being modest in his assessment of the move into Mexico because "some customers" was a bit of an understatement. Everett Smith's grandson, Tom Hauske Jr., had joined Maysteel—a custom-metal fabricator that Smith had owned since the 1960s—right out of college in 1984. He remembered the early and mid 1990s as a time of phenomenal growth for the company. "It really started with the Big Three Detroit OEMs establishing seat-manufacturing facilities south of the border and suggesting that we join them," Hauske recalled. "Segerdahl was instrumental in the start of this growth cycle."[9]

The name of the new subsidiary was Eagle Ottawa de Mexico S.A. de C.V. A 125,000-square-foot facility housed Eagle's initial foray into international cutting.[10]

Callow & Maddox, which employed almost 500 people in two locations, won the *Coventry Evening Telegraph* Business of the Year Award in 1995.

Business awards underline TEC link

FOUR of the seven winners in the Annual Business Awards for Coventry and Warwickshire were linked to the Training and Enterprise Council.

Business of the Year winners in the Coventry Telegraph-backed awards were Callow and Maddox, the Bagington company which dominates the luxury seating market for the car, bus, coach and light rail industries.

Callow and Maddox are involved in YT Quality Training and currently committed to winning recognition as Investors in People. They are also being supported by the TEC under the Business Development Initiative which helps companies manage change.

The company employs 480 people at two factories in Coventry, and their expansion plans would create a further 160 jobs. Sales increased by 72 per cent last year.

The TEC sponsored Business Woman of the Year award went to Claire Davies, aged 37, who is managing director of Mercia Safety Centre Ltd at Hampton Magna, near Warwick.

She designed a Tiny Traveller car seat for new-born babies and worked relentlessly to get it on to the market. The company, which pro-

duces other safety goods such as cot mattresses, custom-fitted child cycle helmets and reflective cycle wear, has been involved in a TEC business review with TEC advisor support.

The title of Small Business of the Year went to TEC nominated Artel Rubber Co. Ltd., of Wellesbourne.

The company has been built up by Graham and Verena Telling and Jeff and Jean Arnold into a specialist company producing long-life reinforced silicone hoses for the truck, bus, train and racing car industries.

They are also considering Investors in People, and serve on the board of the South Warwickshire Business Partnership.

The award for Training Excellence was taken by Coventry building and plumbers merchants Mattersons.

They totally revitalised the 200-year-old company with a sweeping training programme involving every worker, taking in YT Quality Training, a TEC business review and are considering a STEP (Skills Training Employment Progress) programme with Jobs for Coventry.

The awards were presented during a dinner at the de Vere Hotel in Coventry.

Claire Davies receives her award as Business Woman of the Year from Mr Aaron Jones, chairman of Coventry and Warwickshire Training and Enterprise Council.

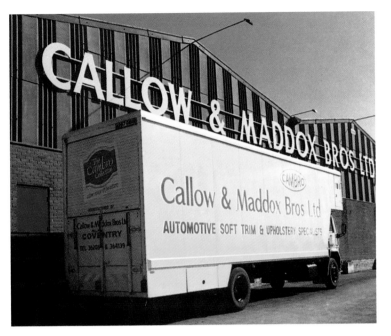

Mr. Segerdahl used to visit us and he said, "You know, guys? This is crazy because we're being given the global business for Ford. We're shipping leather to be cut in Europe. We now have this tannery in Warrington. What if we made the leather in Warrington and got you guys to cut it into car seats for us?"[13]

"[Callow & Maddox] had very modern buildings and lots of land," noted Segerdahl. "It was in a beautiful, industrial part of Coventry. I was saying, 'This is great, let's buy it.' "[14]

On October 17, 1993, the win-win deal was completed. The acquisition made perfect strategic sense. The Pierpoint tannery fed hides into the nearby Callow sewing facility, thus giving Eagle

Next, Segerdahl turned his attention overseas. The Pierpoint & Bryant tannery, which in 1992 was renamed Eagle Ottawa Leather Ltd., had become the linchpin to Eagle's success in Europe. In fact, the British subsidiary was now cranking out leather for Ford on a global level. But Segerdahl wanted to take that extra step toward full service. "We put in a plant to finish the leather [in Warrington]," Segerdahl remembered. "We had come that far, and we said, 'Who in the world is going to cut this leather for us?' "[11]

As it had with Pierpoint and the Berman family before, Eagle found the answer was another company it had already been conducting business with. Callow & Maddox—a sewing company that stitched finished hides into seat covers that were then sent to manufacturers[12]—had already been buying finished leather from Eagle Ottawa Leather Ltd. Significantly, the company, which had been founded in 1945, was a sewer and a cutter of automotive leather. Segerdahl asked Callow & Maddox to do some cutting for Eagle. Unfortunately, as had been the case with Pierpoint & Bryant, Callow & Maddox was struggling. Segerdahl offered to buy the Coventry, England-based company. Neil Dunn, then a Callow & Maddox veteran, remembered the discussions he had with Segerdahl.

Above left: Eagle Ottawa purchased Callow & Maddox in 1993. The company had a well-respected sewing operation in Coventry that supplied leather to British auto companies.

Left: Callow & Maddox's Neil Dunn was appointed CEO of the company in 1998.

Below: A worker packs auto seat covers for Honda. By the 1990s, Eagle Ottawa had customers all over the globe, including hard-to-win Japanese manufacturers.

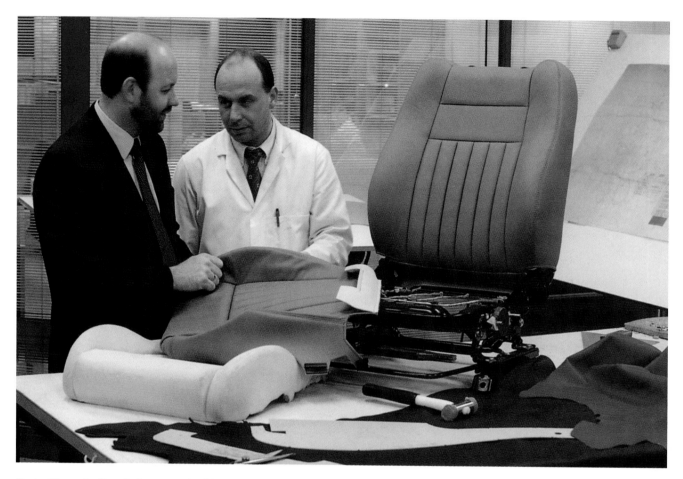

Eagle Ottawa leather designers work with auto designers early in the design process to create seat covers with a wide variety of forms, textures, and finishes.

Ottawa a full-service operation in the U.K. Added value had become the name of the game, and once again Eagle Ottawa had hit a home run.

Prestige also played a role in the purchase. "It brought Eagle Ottawa the stature of owning an old, established sewing company with a very good reputation in the U.K.," Dunn said.

Indeed, at the time of the company's founding after World War II, Coventry was home to English auto manufacturers such as Jaguar, Land Rover, and Austin, with others located nearby. The company's first major car contract came in 1962, when Callow & Maddox earned Triumph's business; the company soon built a plant adjacent to the Triumph factory. Throughout the 1980s, Callow & Maddox continued to expand its pres-

ence in the automobile industry, providing leather to Japanese, American, and British carmakers. In 1989, the company sold its first leather seat covers to Ford.

Still, it needed an infusion of cash. As Dunn put it, the acquisition "gave Callow & Maddox the muscle and financial controls of a global company."[15] After nearly 25 years at the Eagle Ottawa helm, Anders Segerdahl had nearly achieved his goal of transforming Eagle Ottawa into a full-service international automotive leather supplier.

Already a cutter, sewer, and tanner, Eagle Ottawa was being pulled deeper into the supply chain by its customers. Eagle, forever driven by customer service, responded in kind. In its constant quest to think less like a mere supplier and more like an automotive company, Eagle Ottawa's next move was up the design chain.

Soon, Eagle Ottawa designers like Pat Oldenkamp, vice president of design and marketing, were sitting in with car designers as they worked on their new models. "It was really Mr. Segerdahl's vision that Eagle Ottawa could provide more of a service to its customers by supporting the design community and working with the automotive designers up front in new product development," Oldenkamp said. "At that time in 1993, no other automotive upholstery leather company had a design function."[16]

The Other Whitewater

Albert Trostel Packings Ltd. was also expanding its markets in automotive components. The Albert Trostel & Sons subsidiary had been manufacturing its Vamac wheel-bearing seals from its new Whitewater, Wisconsin, facility for two years when in 1992 it introduced a second product. These bonded piston seals caught the attention of General Motors, which signed on as a major client. From 1992 to 1995, Trostel Packings developed and produced 12 bonded piston seal models for GM Power Train. During that same period Trostel Packings began to step up its production of brake diaphragms after successful bids on large-volume contracts with Delphi and Bosch. It had already been manufacturing parts for Bosch braking systems in smaller volumes for 10 years.

"We expanded our diaphragm-producing capability from four injection-molding presses to 14 injection-molding presses," said Tim Baker, who by this time, had been promoted to vice president and general manager of the Polymer Compounding Division. "We were immediately a large player, and we needed space for that."[17]

At the same time, more space was needed to accommodate the increased production of Vamac seals and bonded piston seals. In 1995, the original Whitewater plant space was doubled to 80,000 square feet.

The timing couldn't have been worse. The bonded piston seals, Baker acknowledged, were "a technically difficult product, and we had a customer in GM Power Train that was difficult to work with."[18] Management made a difficult decision to exit the bonded piston seal business, and Trostel Packings was left with a great deal of excess capacity at its state-of-the-art Whitewater facility.

In an attempt to fill capacity at the new plant, some Lake Geneva production was moved to the Whitewater facility, including the Trostel sub-

sidiary's gas-spring parts.[19] Next, Trostel Packings increased production of its polymer compounds. Previously, they had been consumed internally as part of Trostel Packings products; now with the spare capacity, management increased production and hired salespeople in an attempt to sell the compounds directly to other companies.

"They started from scratch," said Joyce Huck. "so they had no customers because they had only made [compounds] for themselves. It started out very slowly."[20]

Trostel Packings' compounding business started to pick up, Huck said, when the Trostel subsidiary hired a salesman who had previously sold rubber equipment and had solid connections with the major rubber companies.[21] "We had an in, and it triggered so fast," Huck said. "Within a year, it was a $1 million business. At two years, it was $2 million."[22] Trostel Packings had turned a near-disaster into yet another major victory.

South Africa and New Blood at the Top

Eagle Ottawa's success was more slowly paced than Trostel Packings' perhaps because it was more deliberate. Every value-added move and global venture that Anders Segerdahl and Eagle Ottawa had made since the end of the 1960s had been in response to customers' needs. Leather cutters and finishers were initially acquired to create added value, and by the 1990s Eagle Ottawa had become a true one-stop shop for automotive leather. The forays into England and Mexico had been made to bring Eagle physically closer to its customers. But those were tentative steps compared with the company's next venture halfway around the world in South Africa. Callow & Maddox's Neil Dunn remembered that a South African tax incentive was the catalyst.

When [Nelson] Mandela came to power, he said to the big guys in the industry—the Fords and the GMs and the BMWs and Mercedes—"I'm glad you're going to manufacture cars in South Africa, [but] understand the game. You are not going to come in here, use cheap labor, and ship product out of the country with no added value other than a job for South Africa. Everything you

GREENER PASTURES

TANNING GREW OUT OF PEOPLE'S NEED to use the land and its creatures to improve their lives. According to legend, Native Americans used every part of the buffalo they killed on the Great Plains.

Yet this process can be taxing on the environment, and Eagle Ottawa, under the direction of Anders Segerdahl, was adamant about developing sound environmental practices. The strong presence of the Green movement in Europe—where Eagle expanded in the 1980s and 1990s—influenced the company's sound environmental practices.[1]

"Everything Eagle Ottawa does is guided by an overriding concern for the environment," read a company report. "Every new product and process is considered not only in the context of how it will improve our leather, but how it will impact the environment."[2]

Eagle Ottawa adopted a three-pronged approach to acting on its environmental concerns. The first was to prevent pollution before it occurred. Second, the company aimed to reduce waste produced by manufacturing. And last, the company took steps to convert waste to a usable by-product.[3]

Eagle Ottawa's environmentally friendly initiatives caused it to de-emphasize the century-old practice of chromium tanning in favor of vegetable tanning agents to produce biodegradable leather.[4] Vegetable tanning was by no means a new concept. Leather had been tanned that way for centuries, but never to the exacting standards of the automobile industry until Eagle Ottawa developed the ingenious process. The challenge was to return to vegetable tanning without harvesting huge stocks of trees.

"The challenge was to make it meet automotive performance specifications, and to do it without using tree bark," according to the company report. "What good, we thought, would it be to respond to one set of earth concerns only to create another by felling trees to tan 'environmental' leather?"[5]

The product Eagle Ottawa created was Phoenix leather. A fruit grown only in Peru gave the leather exceptional beauty, and environmentalists approved of it.[6]

The result was a high-quality leather. The grain retention was superior, as was its sensitivity to heat and cold, a quality that made the leather warmer in the winter and cooler in the summer. Its lower mass contributed to vehicle-weight reduction and improved fuel economy. Further, it was easily recyclable and exceptionally biodegradable.[7]

Anders Segerdahl (right) and David Gould, manager of Newaygo Farms, display the Environmental Quality Award, presented by the Michigan Chamber of Commerce in recognition of Eagle Ottawa's efforts to protect the environment. The award was presented in 1996.

In another groundbreaking, environmentally sound move, Eagle Ottawa broke its dependence on chemical finishing. The firm pioneered the development of water-based finishing, a process that drastically reduced emissions, cutting the release of volatile organic compounds (VOCs) by 99 percent. By 2000, Eagle Ottawa was fast approaching a time when all its leather finishes would be solvent-free.[8]

Eagle Ottawa's ultimate goal was zero discharge toxicity. The company recycled its waste water for continued use and converted its solid waste into a commercial-grade soil enhancer used on the company's Newaygo Farms.[9] Newaygo would play a key role in demonstrating that Eagle Ottawa's leather-making process is environmentally sound:

- Beef industry rawhides are generated as by-products.
- Rawhides are used to produce automotive leather.
- The leather production process generates wastewater that is treated

on-site at Eagle Ottawa's biological treatment facilities. The treatment system operates at 99 percent efficiency producing a high-quality effluent and dewatered biosolids for composting.

- Each year, more than 10,000 tons of biosolids, straw, waste cherries, and pallets are all converted into a rich soil amendment trademarked ReTurn™, which has been applied to the fields at Newaygo Farms biannually since 1994.
- The nutrients and microorganisms in ReTurn™ contribute to healthy crop production while reducing the need for commercial fertilizer and herbicides.
- The cycle is completed when crops grown using ReTurn™ are fed to beef cattle.[10]

Eagle Ottawa was quickly recognized for its conservation efforts. In 1992, Anders Segerdahl received the Theodore Roosevelt Conservation Award at a White House ceremony in honor of the leaner, greener Eagle Ottawa. The Michigan Chamber of Commerce presented its Environmental Quality Award to Eagle Ottawa later that year. It was Segerdahl's leadership and vigilance that developed Eagle Ottawa into the industry's most proactive, environmentally conscious tanner.

"The U.S. Environmental Protection Agency consistently rates our operations highly, setting Eagle Ottawa as the standard-bearer of the industry," announced a company report. "Our efforts have also attracted the attention of leading universities and visits from United Nations-led delegations."[11]

Ultimately, the company's sound environmental record benefited everyone. "This culture was founded on key things that sales and development guys like," said Craig Tonti, Eagle Ottawa's vice president of global sales since 1999, "such as environmental stewardship and the fact that we are the leader around the globe for the environment."[12]

import into the country, there will be a 75 percent duty on it. But I don't want your duty. I want you to create an industry in Africa, export it, and whatever the value of that part or component is, we will give you an export credit called an MITD certificate that you will be able to use to offset against the duty.[23]

There were other motivating factors. South Africa had a thriving manufacturing industry driven by low-cost labor, access to an abundant cattle population, favorable geography, and the presence of multinational companies. Furthermore, BMW, Mercedes Benz, Volvo, Rover, and Mazda already had plants in South Africa. As Segerdahl saw it, this was the perfect opportunity for Eagle Ottawa.

My management was saying that this is going to be beautiful. When I looked at the figures, I thought we had to do it. So we went down there and built a small tannery for about 7,000 to 8,000 hides [per week]. If we were going to grow, we had to follow our customers.[24]

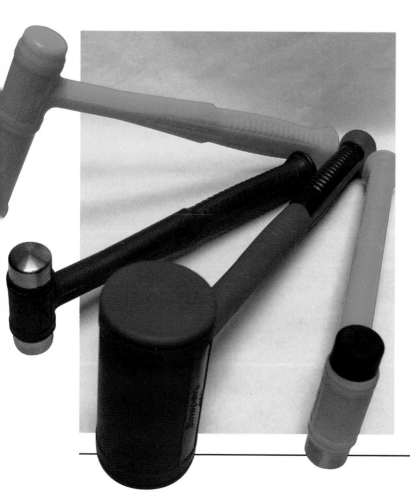

In accordance with the tax-credit provisions, the Bronkhorspruit-based subsidiary, Eagle Ottawa South Africa, took the locally produced raw product and added value to it by tanning, cutting, and sewing it into seat covers, which were then exported to Europe. Although the value of the tax credits would decrease over time, the goals of expansion, customer service, and cost-savings had been achieved.

Packings Restructures

While he entrusted his longtime friend and colleague Anders Segerdahl with the day-to-day operations of Eagle Ottawa, Everett Smith maintained a majority stake in Albert Trostel & Sons' subsidiaries, in addition to a few companies outside the Trostel family. In 1995 he changed the name of his Everett Smith Investments holdings group to the Everett Smith Group, and in 1996 Smith brought his grandson, Tom Hauske Jr., over from Maysteel as vice president of ESG.

With Hauske working out of the ESG/Albert Trostel & Sons headquarters at 800 North Marshall Street and Perry playing a significant role with Albert Trostel Packings Ltd., Smith, at the age of 87, was increasing his family's role in the business he had been running for more than 35 years.

Amid the administrative changes, personnel moves, and Eagle Ottawa's ascendance to the dominant spot in Albert Trostel & Sons' bottom line, the packings subsidiary was now eyed as a major growth opportunity. First, a new name was in order.

"[The name] was no longer appropriate because we weren't manufacturing packings anymore.

Left: Trostel SEG split from the former packings subsidiary in 1997 and focused on cast urethanes for the material handling industry and injection-molded thermoplastics, such as these overmolded hammers.

Opposite: After the split, the former packings subsidiary was renamed Trostel Ltd. Under the leadership of Bob Gamache and then DeWayne Egly, Trostel Ltd. supplied rubber compounds from its PCD facility, built in 1994.

Above: Trostel SEG manufactures open cast polyurethane tires and wheels used in the material handling industry on fork trucks and pallet jacks.

Right: Tom Hauske, Everett Smith's only grandson, moved from Smith's Maysteel holding to the Everett Smith Group in 1996. He came on board as vice president.

Everett Smith's Legacy

Sadly, in 1997, at the age of 88, Everett Smith died. "He had a couple of challenges with his health through the years," Hauske said. "He was really pretty healthy the last seven years." In fact, Smith would still come to the office frequently and was still very engaged in the business right up until his death. His continued presence, Hauske noted, was one of the keys to his companies' ongoing success.[27]

Everett Smith's long-term perspective on business provided stability for the company. His longevity and passion for business were key factors in leading the organization through rapid growth and setting the stage for lasting success. Certainly, there were challenges along the way, but having seen the difficulties the Trostels faced early in his career, he taught us the importance of being financially conservative in the management of our companies.[28]

That name was left over from the leather days," said Perry.[25]

But it wasn't just the nameplate on the buildings that changed. Because the subsidiary's business had yet to mature fully, management decided to restructure. Effective January 1, 1997, "we spun off the urethane and plastics division into a separate subsidiary," Perry said. "It became Trostel SEG, or the Specialty Elastomers Group. Trostel Packings was then renamed Trostel Limited."

Trostel Limited focused on supplying seals to the automotive and appliance industries. SEG concentrated on cast urethanes for the material handling industry and injection-molded thermoplastics, which served the hand-tool, appliance, and automotive markets.[26] Perry, who had been instrumental in turning around SEG's business when it was still a division of Albert Trostel Packings Ltd., was named president of the new subsidiary.

There were two other major reasons for the seamless transition after Smith's death. For one, Smith's determination to keep ESG privately held—just as the Trostels had done for an entire century before he assumed the reins—provided the ideal environment for growth.[29]

"We reinvest in our businesses," Hauske said. "Our companies are allowed to grow through their successes. We encourage and support growth by attracting and empowering talented leaders."[30]

But in the end, as is the case with most success stories in the business world, the continued growth of Smith's companies could be attributed to the people. Each management team provides a great deal of stability for the ESG companies, according to Hauske. "My grandfather said, 'Always hire the best people you can find.' "[31]

Segerdahl's New Role

Perry's sales strategy and restructuring laid the foundation for future growth at Trostel Ltd. and Trostel SEG, but Everett Smith's death changed the company's immediate needs. Anders Segerdahl had been traveling back and forth between Grand Haven and Milwaukee for 30 years. With Smith gone, it was Segerdahl's turn to run the entire Albert Trostel & Sons operation.

"Shortly after Everett Smith's death," Perry said, "Andy took on increased responsibility for the entire Everett Smith Group. Andy asked me to go over and spend two or three years at Eagle Ottawa. He sent me over to learn the leather business and assist the new CEO with corporate development and strategic planning for the business."[32]

Like generations of leaders before him, Perry started in the hide house, visiting packing houses and working with hide buyers. With Segerdahl back in Wisconsin, spending an increasing amount of time tending to his added responsibilities since the death of Everett Smith, and Perry learning the ropes at Eagle Ottawa, it was time to look for Segerdahl's replacement in Grand Haven. "We had people on for a probationary engagement," Segerdahl recalled, "but it was very tough to find [a permanent replacement]." Amazingly, amid all the management movement, Eagle Ottawa managed to earn Toyota's Superior Quality Award.

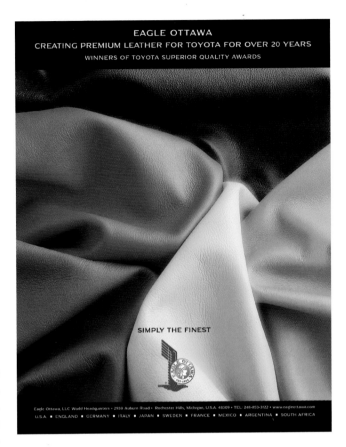

In his 30 years at the helm of Eagle Ottawa, Anders Segerdahl transformed the company from a tanner to a full-service automotive leather cutter, finisher, and designer. In 1998, Eagle Ottawa received the Toyota Superior Quality Award.

New Blood at Eagle

Management took Smith's philosophy of hiring the best man to heart while searching for Segerdahl's replacement at Eagle Ottawa. It also considered the fact that Eagle was no longer just a tanner; it was now a link in the automotive manufacturing chain. In January 1999, Segerdahl recruited Jerry Sumpter as CEO of Eagle Ottawa. Unlike previous executives, Sumpter didn't come from the leather industry. Instead, he was a car man through and through. Before Eagle Ottawa, he had worked at Collins and Aikman, a global manufacturer of interior automotive components.

Sumpter was hired to complete Eagle Ottawa's transformation into a tier-one automotive supplier. Tellingly, his office was in Rochester Hills instead of Grand Haven, giving him easier access to downtown Detroit.

"My background was automotive for the past 14 or 15 years, and when they brought me in, they basically wanted me to continue the transition from a leather supplier to an automotive supplier," Sumpter said. "The difference is that in the leather business the focus was on the leather and the romance of leather. It was a product-focused company. In the automotive business, you have to be focused on the product, but you also have to be very much systems-focused and have a very robust operating system."[33]

Shortly after arriving, Sumpter began recruiting automotive executives to Eagle Ottawa, hoping to instill a supplier mind-set across the company.

"We had great tanners," Perry said. "We didn't have good automotive systems and supply knowledge. Jerry focused on new hires in the sales and marketing and operations group—all with automotive experience."[34] Craig Tonti was one of those new automotive people. Hired in the summer of 1999 as Eagle's vice president of global sales, Tonti had previously worked at United Technologies Automotive, a manufacturer of thermoplastic products for car interiors.

"Jerry was looking to find a way to integrate the sales group with the design group and the product-development group," said Tonti. "Jerry, Randy Perry, and Andy Segerdahl needed one person at the top of the organization chart for all commercial-related activities."[35]

Yet for all of Tonti's and Sumpter's automotive experience, they, like Segerdahl and the Hattons before them, understood and even embraced the company's leather legacy.

"It's a company that is tied to the leather industry and has a lot of heritage," Sumpter said. "Its leaders have had good foresight to get out of certain things that weren't working and into a product that had longevity. It's amazing the phases the company has gone through."[36]

Of course, Segerdahl deserved much of the credit. "He drove that growth," said Tom Hauske Jr. "He listened to the customer. He was very market-driven. There were several very creative joint ventures and long-term buyouts. He developed ways to reduce risk and grow the business during the '90s."[37]

Expansion to Mexico

Trostel Ltd. was subject to the same market pressures and opportunities experienced by Eagle Ottawa. First among them was the reduced cost of operating in select foreign markets. Eagle Ottawa, through its locations in Mexico and South Africa, had already taken advantage of this economic reality. Manufacturing shifts also provided better access to global markets.

By the late 1990s, Bob Gamache and Trostel Ltd. sought similar opportunities in Mexico. By locating facilities in Mexico, Trostel Ltd. management hoped to reap both of these benefits—especially the cost savings. In many manufacturing

Eagle Ottawa opened its South African subsidiary in 1996 to take advantage of an abundant local hide market and a growing automotive supply market that primarily served European OEMs.

industries the last real sales price increase had come in 1998; in some sectors of the manufacturing economy, prices were actually experiencing deflation.

"When you're working in the world of automotive or appliances, there is no such thing as a price increase," Gamache said. "The only way you can get a price increase is when the product goes obsolete and you get a new one, or you do something different. You have to innovate."[38]

Before expanding into Mexico, Trostel Ltd. studied its sister company Eagle Ottawa and other companies that had relocated operations in that country and soon discovered a basic set of principles that governed success. One was caution. Too many companies had relocated virtually all of their

manufacturing to Mexico without really understanding the market and local culture. In many cases, these companies lost huge investments before they adapted to their host country. Trostel would not make this mistake. Ultimately, the company decided the best location for a new facility was just over the border from McAllen, Texas, in Reynosa, Mexico.[39]

Above: Trostel Ltd. and SEG staffers pride themselves on developing close technical relationships with customers.

Below: Eagle Ottawa engineers and designers during various stages of the process. The company can produce almost any shade of leather in many styles and textures, to meet a client's needs.

The company planned its expansion carefully, initially producing only a limited run in its Mexican facility. "We built a plant that we could manage and support technically," Gamache said. "We found a capable Mexican manager, picked out a couple of good, technical people that we had that wanted to relocate, and then used the one/one process: one type of press, one type of compound."[40]

As Segerdahl had with Eagle Ottawa, Gamache and Trostel Ltd. developed an international strategy and then acted deliberately. As with Segerdahl and Eagle Ottawa, Gamache and Trostel Ltd.'s strategy led to enormous success.

SEG Steps Out on Its Own

As the 1990s drew to a close, Trostel SEG was finding its footing as a separate subsidiary of Albert Trostel & Sons. The company's leading product line, which represented about 50 percent of sales, consisted of solid tires and wheels for electrically powered lift trucks, according to Thomas Mahnke, SEG's market development manager of castable urethanes.[41] Additionally, SEG made rollers for elevators and escalators, components for railroad and over-the-road vehicles, track pads for construction equipment, tool covers, and a variety of products for industrial and automotive applications.[42]

SEG manufactured these items in its Lake Geneva plant primarily using polyurethanes, which offered a number of advantages over traditional rubber products. Thermoplastics offered more diversity and economy than either leather or rubber. And they were environmentally sound. Thermoplastic resin products were essentially reusable and recyclable, giving them enormous advantages over other prod-

The team at Trostel SEG boasts technical competency in both urethane casting and molding.

ucts. According to Michael Kirst, SEG's operations manager, the range of products made from plastics ran the gamut from replacement bones to engine components, gears, and space shuttle parts.[43]

SEG employed two core polyurethane technologies—injection molding and casting. At first Trostel used only casting, whereby polyurethane was melted and poured into a mold. Except for some trimming and curing, the pouring and cooling was the extent of the production, a relatively simple and inexpensive process.[44]

SEG moved into injection molding when the rubber operation was employed to help the Bosch company develop a dampening device for a metal insert. Determining that the best solution would be the new technique of injection molding, the company purchased a used machine and began producing the part for Bosch.[45]

Injection molding used hot thermoplastic resin that was forced under great pressure into a mold where it cooled and solidified. The precision process required much more expensive equipment and yielded products—like plastic tool covers—of higher quality in larger quantities than those produced by cast urethane. The demand for precision products grew so quickly that by the late 1990s, injection molding had become a very important component of SEG's business.[46]

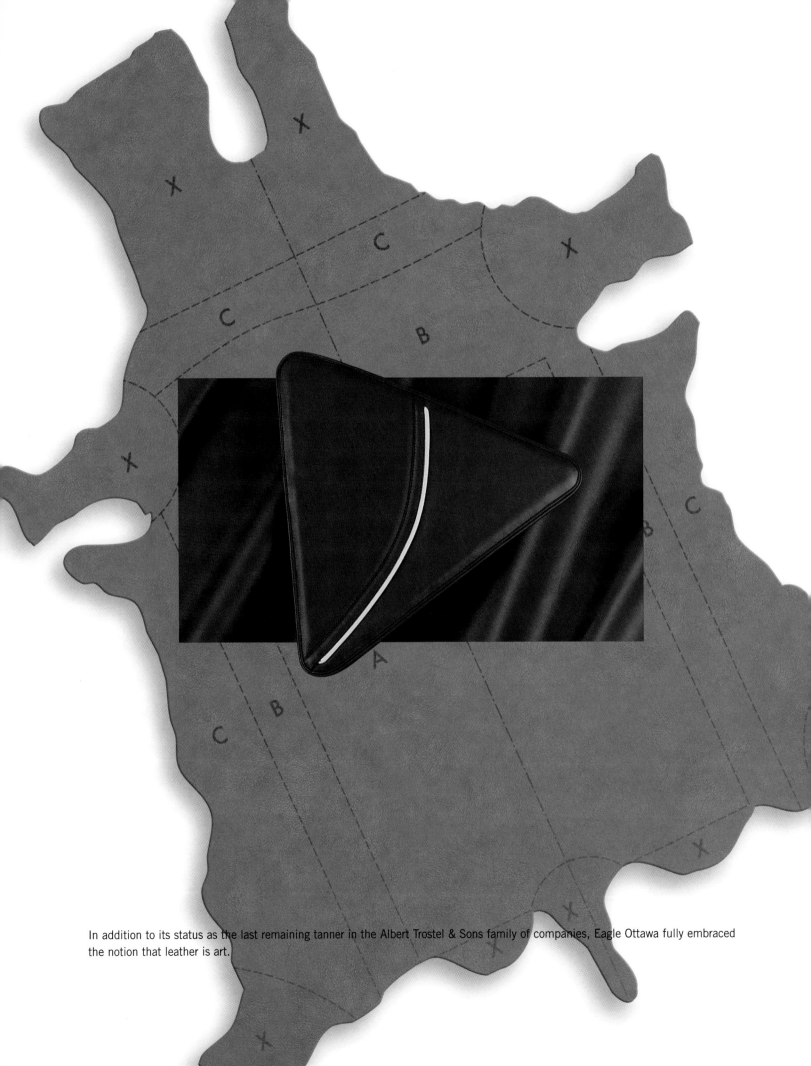

In addition to its status as the last remaining tanner in the Albert Trostel & Sons family of companies, Eagle Ottawa fully embraced the notion that leather is art.

CHAPTER TEN

THE DAWN OF A
NEW MILLENNIUM

2000 AND BEYOND

*We run a very decentralized operation. We want to attract and retain
the best leaders that we can find. My relationship with the CEO at Eagle
Ottawa and Trostel Ltd. and SEG is extremely important. We want to
make sure they understand we're here to support them.*

—Randy Perry, President and COO, Albert Trostel & Sons

THE NEW MILLENNIUM BEGAN just as the previous one ended for the Albert Trostel & Sons family of companies—with a flurry of activity. Eagle Ottawa wasted no time expanding further—this time to South America. To improve its access to less-expensive hides and an experienced labor pool, Eagle established a leather cutting and finishing joint venture with Curtiembres Fonseca. Eagle Ottawa Fonseca immediately took advantage of Argentina's relatively low-cost leather.

Eagle Ottawa had already developed a relationship with Fonseca, according to Jerry Sumpter. Fonseca had been supplying Eagle's North American operations with tanned materials. The next step was obvious to Sumpter and Randy Perry, who at this time, had become the company's resident strategist, evaluating prospective regions and products and creating joint ventures.

"We saw an opportunity to create a joint venture," Sumpter said. "We took the material that they were supplying to North America—or at least some of it—and finished and cut it there into parts. We utilized the Argentine capabilities and costs, which were quite good, to give us a competitive advantage."[1]

"It's a higher-grade leather than furniture leather, for instance, because of its wear characteristics," added Perry. "Argentina proved to be an ideal location because of the abundance of hides."

Indeed, according to Perry, Argentina has a population of 13 million cattle, but only 10 percent of these hides are usable for automotive upholstery. That small percentage, 1.3 million usable hides, was a significant high-quality supply.[2]

With facilities in Argentina, Mexico, England, South Africa, and throughout North America, Eagle Ottawa seemingly had the globe covered, but Sumpter would continue to adhere closely to Anders Segerdahl's principles of customer service and proximity.

South of the Border Ltd.

After taking time to plan carefully its initial foray outside of the U.S., Trostel Ltd. began construction on its Reynosa, Mexico, plant in 2001. As was the case with Eagle Ottawa's South African venture, Bob Gamache was drawn south of the border by a tax credit.

We needed a low-cost location for certain products that had matured [but] we wanted to keep.

In 2001, Eagle Ottawa opened this plant in Szolnok, Hungary, to be closer to some of its customers. By 2003, employees at the facility were cutting 6,000 to 7,000 hides per week.

Like his predecessor, DeWayne Egly focused on innovation and customer service to continue the growth of Trostel Ltd.

There was good product, but we needed something else with it. I commissioned Bruce Betters, our VP of finance, to find our place in Mexico, and he did a study. We decided that we would do a maquilidora [tax credit] on the [other side of the] McAllen, Texas border.[3]

Under maquilidora guidelines, Gamache explained, "everything you bring in, you have to bring out. And you're only taxed on what is actually done in Mexico and not on the entire product."[4]

From the Reynosa plant, Trostel Ltd. began to produce brake products, washing machine products, and, Gamache said, 12 million to 15 million gas spring seals per year.

Company research had shown that keeping the Mexican operations simple was the key to success. "Those who tried to throw everything down there thinking that the labor cost would save them failed," Gamache noted. In Trostel Ltd.'s case, he noted, as many as 200 cavity tools were used in the manufacture of these items, but "the process was identical, so the training time was the whole key."[5]

As Bruce Betters characterized the Mexican operation, "We wouldn't be as competitive on the rubber side without it."[6]

Not long after the Reynosa facility opened, Bob Gamache retired after 25 years with the company. In 2001, Albert Trostel executives recruited DeWayne Egly to succeed Gamache. Egly had spent 25 years with Dana, a global leader in the design, engineering, and manufacture of value-added products for automotive and commercial vehicles. Egly was drawn to the company for several reasons.

I liked the idea of a private company. I liked the idea that it was a company that had been around awhile. I was interested in being the president of a company, and I didn't think it was going to happen in Dana. So I thought this would be a good opportunity.[7]

The company offered Egly plenty of opportunity; Trostel Ltd. in turn benefited from Egly's experience. "DeWayne had an excellent career at Dana," said Gamache, who stayed on three months past his retirement date to help Egly acclimate. "He brought with him a lot of very good management skills."[8]

Those skills and experience would be tested as Egly faced some immediate challenges. "[Trostel] had a good reputation in the marketplace," he said, "but they were dealing with the cost-competitive nature of the marketplace."[9]

Egly went right to work, asking some basic questions. About internal operations, Egly asked, "What does our manufacturing look like? Is it really lean? What do we do to get the cost structure in line? Are we properly organized for it?"[10]

The questions about external relationships were perhaps more difficult to answer. "What do we sell to the marketplace?" Egly asked. "What [should] our market leadership role be?"

Egly's response particularly to the question on leadership, would have made his short-term mentor Bob Gamache proud. In two words, Egly's answer was "customer intimacy."[11]

We looked at how we could focus on our current customer base and expand our products. Yet, at the same time, we said, "We really need to grow much faster than we can with just our own customers." So we set up a few things for both organic and inorganic growth—what products to look for and what technologies to go after.[12]

Egly's two-pronged approach to innovate while keeping customers satisfied suited Trostel Ltd.'s staple item, the seal, very well. After all, the product had undergone many changes since the

packings division launched production of synthetic rubber seals in 1948. To continue to stay abreast of technology shifts into the new millennium, Egly added a vice president of technology position to his organization.

"Efficiency is everything; quality is everything," Gamache remarked. "You have to keep upgrading, improving, and changing. We've maintained margins on some products with no price increases over 15 years, and the only way you do that is through technology."[13]

And it was only through technology that Trostel Ltd. was able to maintain a lead over the bulk of the competition. Charlie Hicks, an independent sales rep who began handling Trostel products in 1986, had definite opinions about Trostel and its competition. "There are thousands of molded-rubber companies in the United States," Hicks said. "But

Trostel Ltd. has come a long way since its early incarnation as Albert Trostel Packings Ltd. No longer a division of Albert Trostel & Sons, the separate company moved from leather to rubber long ago. Below is Trostel Ltd.'s Whitewater, Wisconsin, molding plant.

there are only five or six worldwide that make precision rubber products bonded to metal, and Trostel is one of those. Most people in Lake Geneva don't realize that General Motors couldn't build a car tomorrow if Trostel stopped making what they make. On a front-wheel-drive General Motors car, we have six seals in wheel bearings alone."[14]

SEG's Bold Move

Four years after stepping out from the Trostel Ltd. shadow as a company in its own right, Trostel SEG made its first major move. In 2001, an additional 30,000 square feet was added to its Lake Geneva facility to house thermoplastic production, giving cast urethane 20 percent more space for automation. Thomas Sloane, who joined SEG as president and CEO the same year it split from Trostel Packings, was, like DeWayne Egly, interested in innovation to meet customer needs.

"It's always changing because the technology evolves," Sloane said. "[Customers] want vehicles to carry higher loads and go faster, or they're looking for economical means by which to solve material handling or construction problems."[15]

SEG worked diligently to meet those demands. "I believe we're second to none in the industry as far as our technical capability," said Michael Kirst, SEG's operations manager. "We're not necessarily the biggest, but we're the best in our niches of insert molding and dual-shot applications. Our ownership is very supportive in supplying capital."[16]

Trostel SEG's thermoplastics serve the automotive, small-engine, and power-tool industries. Conventional, insert, and dual-shot molding technologies are used to produce them.

SEG's oldest business, cast urethane, was still its most lucrative, as it had been since the 1950s. Its largest market was and continues to be material handling—tires and wheels for forklifts and pallet jacks. Sloane explained the technology involved.

It's an open-cast process where a metal rim is prepared through an extensive preparation process. A variety of chemicals are mixed in precision ratios, and the mold itself has to be heated. Then it is poured and goes through a curing process. It is de-molded. Typically, it is a 16-hour cycle.[17]

Cast urethane applications were important in the trucking and construction industries, but in the early 2000s, Trostel SEG's biggest customers were material-handling equipment manufacturers such as the Raymond Corporation and the Crown Corporation. An economic downturn that reduced demand from the material industry hurt, but SEG bounced back.

"We've done an awful lot within our organization to reinvent ourselves and make our manufacturing processes ever more lean and more competitive," Sloane said. "[We have] positioned ourselves to weather this storm, and as the economy begins to come back, to be more successful than maybe we previously thought possible."[18]

Despite its dominance of Trostel SEG's business at the turn of the millennium, the cast urethane products had matured, Sloane said, and the company cast an eye toward the rapidly growing thermoplastics market. With these injection-molded items, SEG served the automotive and hand-tool industries. SEG's customers included Snap On Tools, Strattec, and Briggs and Stratton, for which it manufactures fuel filters for lawn-mower engines.[19]

Once again, an investment in technology paved the way, according to Kirst. The company purchased Engel injection molding machines, which allowed SEG engineers technical flexibility with rotary, shuttle, horizontal, and vertical capabilities.[20] The new process of course, required capital investment.

"That was one of the major reasons why I came to the group," Kirst said. "I'd heard about their dedication. I saw it when I interviewed, and I believed in their philosophy of growing the opportunity as a

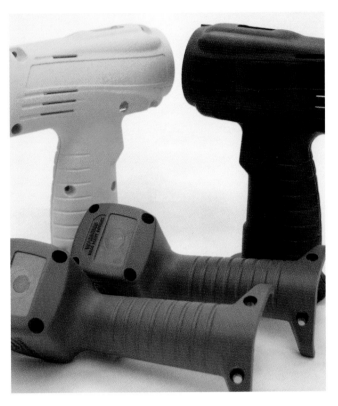

SEG's glass-filled nylon cordless drill and impact wrench housings are used primarily by auto mechanics.

family, not as a corporation. What's unique about this corporation, from my perspective, is that they empower the managers within the division to lead to their own destiny."[21]

Even with the maturity in its cast urethane line, Trostel SEG, as well as Trostel Ltd. continued to have significant growth potential. Thus the rubber and plastics companies served as a balance to the larger Eagle Ottawa.

Eagle: The 800-Pound Gorilla

Despite the growth of SEG and Trostel Ltd., Eagle Ottawa was still the largest of the three Albert Trostel & Sons companies. The first few years of the new millennium saw Eagle Ottawa continuing to build on the growth that Jerry Sumpter inherited from Anders Segerdahl in 1999. In 2001, Eagle opened a cutting plant in Szolnok, Hungary. "That's where the big boys want us to be because they have more favorable rates of pay in the Eastern bloc countries," said Neil Dunn, who had been appointed managing director of Eagle's European operations. The hides were tanned in England, but cut in Hungary.[22]

Proximity to tier 1 automotive suppliers, who were beginning to locate plants in Eastern Europe was another compelling reason for launching operations in Hungary,[23] said Randy Perry, who by this time had pulled back from the day-to-day field operations, and returned to Milwaukee to join the corporate structure of Albert Trostel & Sons.

"This cutting facility will be a major cutting facility in Europe," said Dunn. "We have two or three presses in there, and by early 2003, they were cutting between 6,000 to 7,000 hides a week."[24]

The big news for Eagle Ottawa was the growth of its South African operations. "The market down there is about $250 million for automotive leather upholstery," Perry said. "We have a third of that market now, and that really supplies the European continent."[25] Eagle's South African facility supplied automotive seat leather to BMW, Audi, Volkswagen, Volvo, Range Rover, and Mazda.[26]

The South African operations were managed by Danie Venter, who started working with Eagle Ottawa in 2002. "I think our facility in South

Africa is particularly good," said Venter. "It's a very modern factory." In 2002 the company opened a temporary cutting plant in Centurion, South Africa, while nearby it built a new factory which Venter claimed would be "the best in the Southern Hemisphere."[27]

In Mexico, Eagle's business was bursting at the seams. By 2002, the company had its 120,000-square-foot facility in Juarez and was leasing a second, 75,000-square-foot facility. By the end of 2002, Eagle Ottawa de Mexico S.A. de C.V. was processing 39,500 hides per week, 3,000 of which were finished. The cut part was sent to a sewing manufacturer, according to Kevin Velik, a third-generation Albert Trostel & Sons employee who directed Eagle's Mexican operations.[28] From the Mexico facilities, Velik said, Eagle shipped to central and eastern Mexico, as well as locations in the United States, Canada, and Asia.[29] In 2003, the company built a 130,000-square-foot plant, employing about 2,000.

For Eagle Ottawa, the Mexican, South African, and Hungarian locations—as well as those in Argentina and England—all signified a strategic decision to move closer to the company's customers and

Above right: Randy Perry joined Albert Trostel & Sons in 1992 and over the next decade worked for Trostel SEG, Trostel Ltd., and Eagle Ottawa in operations roles. In 2002, he was elected president and chief operating officer of Albert Trostel & Sons.

Below: Eagle Ottawa boasts a one-third share of South Africa's $250 million automotive leather upholstery market. Eagle's South African facility supplies seat leather to Audi, BMW, Mazda, Range Rover, Volkswagen, and Volvo.

to become a player in the world market. The moves paid off. In 2002, Eagle Ottawa generated $550 million in revenue. Albert Trostel & Sons even called Eagle the company's "800-pound gorilla."[30]

Still, the company was eyeing a major push into the largest market in the world—China. There were two reasons. One was China's sheer size; the second was yet another attractive combination of low-cost labor and proximity to customers. "Our next big move will be China," Perry said in 2002. "We have been researching China for the last 12 months. What's happening is, the automotive market in China is continuing to grow. The leather penetration isn't significant yet, but if you believe half of what they say in terms of global demand for vehicles, China is a place where we have to be."[31]

In 2003, Eagle Ottawa had already hired a Chinese national to work with a team from the company and plan the opening of a Chinese operation. Later that year, the company was up and running with a new manufacturing facility. "The primary reason we've gone to China is really to serve that market," Perry said. "We don't intend to export back to the States from there. We intend to serve the domestic market there, but also serve Toyota, Nissan, and Honda back to Japan."[32]

Even as the company continued to extend its global reach, Eagle Ottawa executives worked to organize the operation in a way that made sense to the auto industry.

"Our management style has really migrated over the last four or five years from a very decentralized management style to a very centralized management

Right: Eagle Ottawa's China team operated from a transitional facility in Shanghai in 2003. Dinggui Gao (seated, third from left), was the operation's general manager, and Cary Bean (seated, third from right) was the Asian sales vice president.

Below: Eagle Ottawa broke ground on a manufacturing facility—depicted here by a computer illustration—in April 2004 to serve China, the world's largest market.

style," said company controller Patrick Roeser. "Now we have operations people who function globally rather than just for a plant or region, and we have systems that function globally. Our information-systems software is common throughout the world. The financial reporting we use is common throughout the world. I think it has really contributed enormously to our profitability."[33]

Of course, China would also generate revenue for Eagle Ottawa. Perry expected Eagle Ottawa to grow even further, thanks to its presence in China, but he added, "A $550 million company is not likely to become a $1 billion company solely on the shoulders of leather tanning products."[34] For Eagle Ottawa, future growth would come in other areas.

From the Trostels and Smith to Segerdahl and Perry

Innovation, but not at the expense of customer service; autonomy for division and subsidiary heads, but not at the expense of investment and other support; international ventures for the sake of competitive labor, but never at the expense of high-quality products—these were the hallmarks of the Albert Trostel & Sons business, passed down from generation to generation. Albert O. Trostel Jr. embraced these principles, as did his friend and successor Everett Smith.

After Jerry Sumpter had assumed the presidency of Eagle Ottawa, and Anders Segerdahl had settled in as chairman and CEO of Albert Trostel & Sons it was time to choose a president. In just over a decade with Albert Trostel & Sons, Randy Perry had received a thorough education in all of the company's businesses—from the sale of polyurethane wheels to the purchase of Argentinian hides for car seats. In 2002, Perry was elected president and chief operating officer of Albert Trostel & Sons and began to focus on the long-term strategic direction of this diversified manufacturing company. Perry understood that his role was to lead the company into the future, but also remain true to its traditions. In that sense, he had been taught well by his mentor, Anders Segerdahl, who had learned a great deal about operations from Albert O. Trostel Jr.

Segerdahl had laid the foundation for Perry. Although many strategic decisions were made inside the operating companies, Smith stayed

When he assumed the presidency of Albert Trostel & Sons in 2002, Randy Perry (left) cultivated relationships with Eagle Ottawa's Jerry Sumpter and the leaders of the company's other subsidiaries.

deeply involved in the business until his death five years prior to Perry's assumption of leadership. Smith's overall vision and energy enabled the companies to evolve as they did. Without Smith's blessing, Anders Segerdahl could not have successfully focused Eagle Ottawa on automotive leather. And without Smith's backing and Segerdahl's leadership, Trostel Ltd. and Trostel SEG would not have successfully evolved from industrial leather to high-tech manufacturers of thermoplastic and rubber parts.

The modern company, including its subsidiaries, is a testament to Smith's creativity and management style. He believed in hiring the best people possible and in giving them the autonomy to push their businesses forward. When Anders

Segerdahl first recommended divesting unprofitable product lines at Eagle Ottawa and focusing on automotive seat covers, Smith deferred. In this way, he drew from the strengths, foresight, and intelligence of others to build a business whose three companies generated about $650 million in revenue during 2002.

"Each of the companies within Albert Trostel & Sons has its own culture," Perry said. "But having worked in all three of them, they are not dissimilar."[35] What unifies them, Perry said, is the quality of their leadership.

We run a very decentralized operation. We want to attract and retain the best leaders that we can find. My relationship with the CEO at Eagle Ottawa and Trostel Ltd. and SEG is extremely important. We want to make sure they understand we're here to support them. We make sure they have access to capital so they can

show their product and process capabilities to customers. We give them the latitude that they need to feel as if they're entrepreneurs with their own businesses, and create that entrepreneurial environment that allows them to motivate their teams. We've got financial targets that we set, and we've got expectations for those, but we really leave it up to the CEOs to develop their strategies and come to us with a plan and an execution strategy, and then we're there to support them.[36]

Of course, this autonomy and entrepreneurial environment is reinforced by the fact that this successful, forward-looking company has never seriously considered going public. Jim Orth, vice president of finance for the Everett Smith Group, cited the company's private status as a competitive advantage.

"We can have a much longer-range view," Orth said. "Decisions tend to be made trying to look five, 10, 15 years ahead, which is probably part of the reason the company has been able to adapt to changes over its relatively long history. Also, there's a lot of emphasis on the balance sheet, as well as income. Again, we look forward 10 or 15 years on

In 2003, Trostel SEG acquired Techniplas Inc., an Iowa-based manufacturer and designer of thermoplastic injection-molded products such as these vehicle end caps (inset) and running boards.

Above: Thomas Sloane joined Trostel SEG just after it spun off from Trostel Ltd. in 1997. With the addition of Techniplas, Trostel SEG generated $30 million in revenue in 2003.

Right: Trostel Ltd.'s staple product continues to be seals.

Trostel SEG generated a combined $80 million in revenue—about 15 percent of Eagle's annual revenues. While $80 million was respectable, executives knew that Albert Trostel & Sons' future growth depended on the continued growth of Trostel Ltd. and SEG.

"We have a very focused acquisition strategy in the rubber and plastics platform that will provide additional scale for their future growth," Perry said.[38] In July 2003, the strategy was put to good use when Trostel SEG purchased Techniplas Inc., an Iowa-based designer and manufacturer of thermoplastic injection-molded products. SEG nearly doubled its annual revenue in one fell swoop, from $17 million to $30 million.[39]

"The acquisition of Techniplas represents an important step in our strategy to seek opportunities that expand our rubber- and plastic-molding platform," said Perry. "The combination of Techniplas and Trostel SEG will provide a much broader range of thermoplastic manufacturing capabilities, and further diversify our product lines and markets served."[40]

scheduled payments so we have a very serviceable amount of principal to pay. We are able to grow by managing our balance sheet."[37]

The Future

When the company was formed in 1858, it was a local tannery. By the early 2000s it had evolved so far from its original core business that Albert Gottlieb Trostel would hardly recognize it. Yet in the modern industrial world, where change is the only constant, this progress was a sign of strength. Senior executives from Eagle Ottawa, Trostel Ltd., and Trostel SEG remained focused on their customers and markets; otherwise, growth would be unlikely. By 2002 Trostel Ltd. and

The markets Techniplas served at the time of the merger included the heavy truck, automotive, fitness, medical, and general industrial markets.

"The acquisition provides the combined companies with the scale necessary in today's business environment to take advantage of growth opportunities and further emerge as a leader in the thermoplastics industry," added SEG President Thomas Sloane.[41]

As Techniplas founder Tom Grimes put it succinctly, the merger was "a great fit."[42]

Although the company had grown with the acquisition, SEG still had a lot of potential. Niche products serving the hand-tool industry were a recent development. "We're looking at ways to reduce shock and vibration," said Sloane, who added that ergonomics was another consideration in product development.[43]

And despite their split into separate companies, Sloane said that Trostel SEG and Trostel Ltd. would continue to collaborate. "We work together on things that are primarily their specialty, but [we'll provide] plastic parts as a part of an assembly. We do that primarily for the appliance industry."[44]

SEG and Ltd. were on the same upward trajectory. "Within five years," Bruce Betters said in late 2002, "I'd like to see those businesses double in size—to actually have some critical mass to them."[45]

Through the purchase of Techniplas and some internal gains over the previous year, Trostel SEG and Trostel Ltd. generated $100 million in 2003, so Betters' forecast would yield some impressive numbers. But Randy Perry was even more optimistic. "I'd like to see our rubber and plastics group at a $250 million size, which would be getting close to half the size of our leather business [at Eagle Ottawa]."[46]

For Trostel Ltd.'s part, DeWayne Egly's strategy consisted of fixing over-capacity issues and identifying new customers and markets.[47] In Mexico, the company's operations had steadily expanded. By 2003, its products ranged from custom seals to precision moldings that could be found in cars, washing machines, and gas springs.

For all the talk of maturity, Eagle Ottawa continues to flourish—and grow. "Our long-range projections are for growth, and we continue to see very, very good opportunities around the world," said Jerry Sumpter. "Our best opportunities for

In addition to Ford, Eagle Ottawa leather can be found in Chrysler, GM, Acura, BMW, Mercedes, Nissan, Honda, Audi, Land Rover, Saab, and Volvo cars.

growth are probably in China and Europe, which is where we had the least market share."[48]

Although the company is privately held, Perry estimated that sales for 2003 were in the vicinity of $580 million. By 2004, its seat covers could be found in Cadillac, Chrysler, Ford, General Motors, Land Rover, Audi, BMW, Mercedes, Saab, Volvo, Acura, Honda, Infiniti, Nissan, Lexus, and Toyota models.

The list will continue to grow, as will Eagle Ottawa's participation. Now, in addition to revenue forecasts, company executives talk about market share.

"We've been able to capitalize on global markets and really hit a string of home runs in the

Above: Anders Segerdahl has been on the Board of Directors of Albert Trostel & Sons since 1962, and was elected president of the company in the late 1980s. Today, he is chairman and CEO of the Albert Trostel & Sons operation.

Below: Trostel Ltd. introduced precision compounding to its arsenal of capabilities.

last two or three years," Craig Tonti said in 2002. "I think we'll be able to grow at the impressive rate we've been growing for at least another year or two, then at that point, we'll have approximately 30 percent of the global leather market for automotive seating applications."[49]

According to Perry, once Eagle Ottawa reaches 30 percent to 35 percent market share, it will be time to look at opportunities beyond its core business.

Once we hit that level, in order to keep the company growing, we're going to need to look at acquisitions and possibly get into other components. How do we leverage that global platform and that automotive team into something that we know? We've looked at seating components. We've looked at ways to develop a strategy that would take more manufacturing out of our customers' hands because as the market consolidates, and the tier 1 suppliers look to become interior integrators, they will get further removed from component manufacturing. What is less value-added for them, something like sewing, is natural for us.[50]

For all of the added value that sewing, cutting, and designing provides Eagle's customers, the company remains committed to leather, said Jerry Sumpter.

We're a leather company. Our commitment to this product is strong, as is its history. It is a product like no other. It is natural. It changes daily. It changes by season. It changes by country. It changes by cows, by steers, by whatever type of raw material you buy. So while we want to be a very well-run operating system, we don't want to lose the art of leather, and what leather means to people when they feel it and touch it and smell it.[51]

A Century of Transition

Like all large businesses, the story of Albert Trostel & Sons is much more than a story of products and machines and factories. It is the saga of people combining their foresight and intelligence into a successful enterprise. It is the story of a city, Milwaukee, and the influence of German immigrants on their new land. It is the story of perseverance and flexibility in the face of a changing world and a devotion to the customers who ultimately determine in which direction the company goes.

Today, beyond the balance sheet, company leaders predict that Albert Trostel & Sons will prosper in the future by maintaining its values, planning for the long term, and continuing to breed an entrepreneurial spirit among its managers and operating executives.

It's a spirit that has long helped the company retain good people. Thomas Mahnke has been with the company since 1964. "The reason that I've worked at this one company for this length of time is the fact that it is always changing, always moving forward," Mahnke said. "There have been many opportunities and challenges that I probably would not have had working for some other company."[52]

The Marshall Street office, where Anders Segerdahl, Randy Perry, and Tom Hauske Jr. work. From this historic building, they oversee Eagle Ottawa, Trostel Ltd., and Trostel SEG.

"We have been very fortunate to have leaders like Smith and Segerdahl at the helm of Albert Trostel & Sons for the last 40 years," said Perry. "Smith provided a patient, long-term perspective and the capital to fuel our growth. Segerdahl has incredible long-term vision and seized opportunities to position the companies to achieve that vision. His vision propelled Albert Trostel & Sons from a small regional manufacturer to a truly global competitor. Andy taught me how to balance fiscal conservatism with prudent entrepreneurial risk-taking—a legacy we will continue to promote throughout the organization."[53]

"It's very important for us to determine our own destiny," Anders Segerdahl said. "We are growing all over the world, and we have the customers. We have a good strategic plan, and we have strong people in the companies to make the next step."[54]

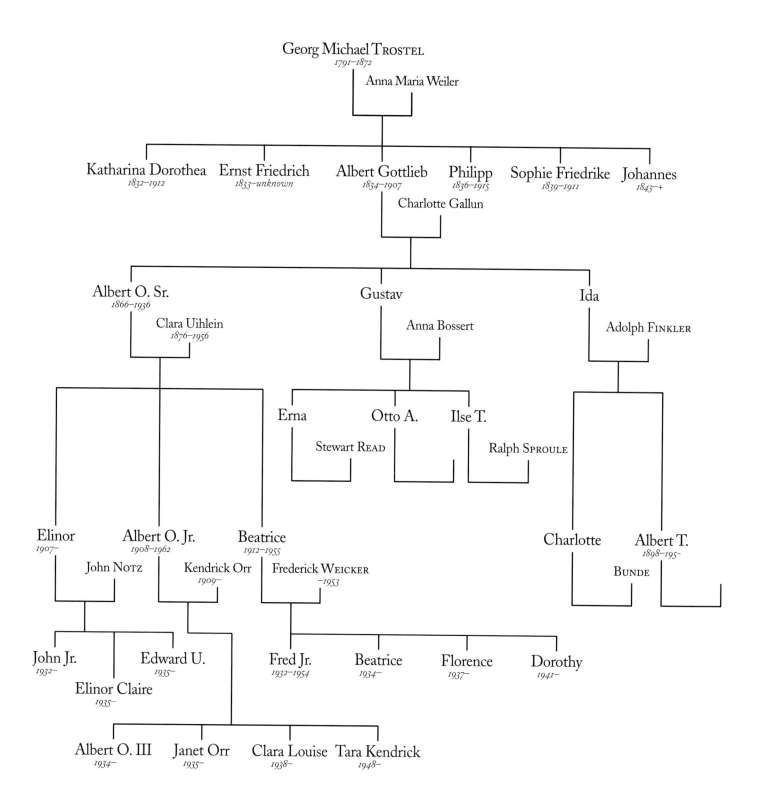

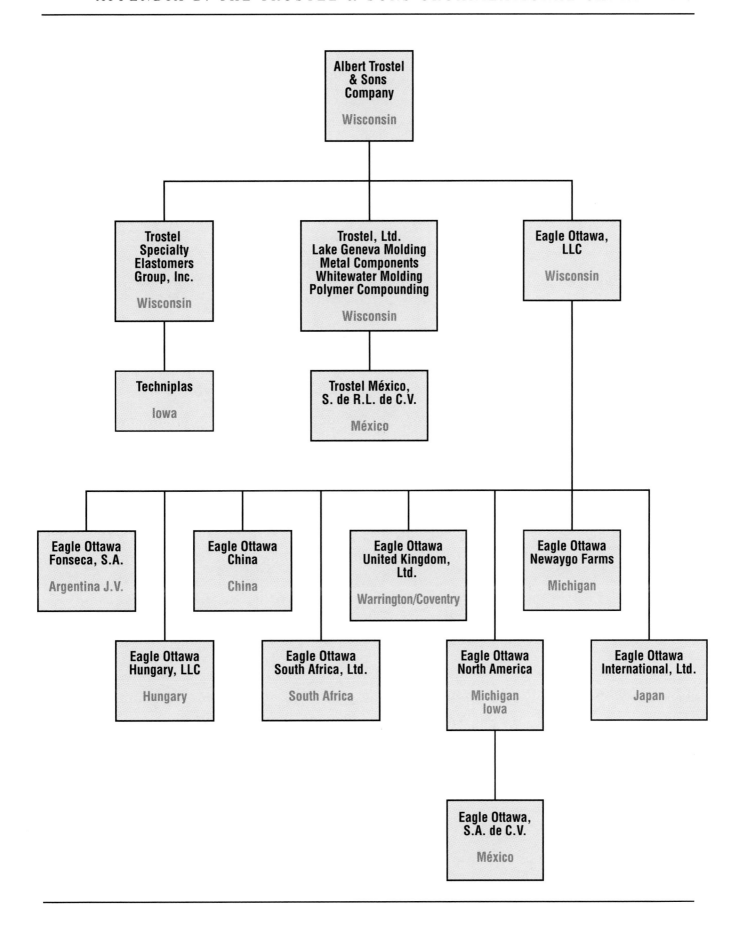

NOTES TO SOURCES

Chapter One

1. "Albert Trostel & Sons," company history, Albert Trostel & Sons company archives, 1.
2. Ibid.
3. Ibid.
4. "Manufactures," *Milwaukee Sentinel*, 19 January 1874.
5. *The Successful American*, photocopy in Albert Trostel & Sons company archives, December 1901, 754.
6. "Albert Trostel & Sons," 3.
7. Trostel Family Tree, Albert Tostel & Sons company archives.
8. Robert Shea, "The German 1848 Revolution—German-American Dimension," http://www.serve.com/shea/germusa/1848.htm.
9. *Successful American*, 754.
10. Shea, "The German 1848 Revolution."
11. Ibid.
12. Ibid.
13. Ibid.
14. Ellen Langill and Dave Jensen, *Milwaukee 150: The Greater Milwaukee Story* (Milwaukee, WI: Milwaukee Publishing Group , 1996), 23.
15. Robert W. Wells, *Yesterday's Milwaukee* (Miami, FL: E.A. Seemann Publishing, Inc., 1976), 17.
16. Ibid., 122.
17. Langill and Jensen, *Milwaukee 150*, 23.
18. Ibid.
19. Wells, *Yesterday's Milwaukee*, 19.
20. Ibid.
21. Bayrd Still, *Milwaukee: The History of a City* (Madison, WI: The State Historical Society of Wisconsin), 186.
22. Ibid., 186–87.
23. Langill and Jensen, *Milwaukee 150*, 32.
24. Peter C. Welsh, *Tanning in the United States to 1850: A Brief History* (Washington, D.C.: Museum of History and Technology, Smithsonian Institution, 1964), 3.
25. Still, *Milwaukee: The History of a City*, 187.
26. Welsh, *Tanning in the United States*, 15.
27. Still, *Milwaukee: The History of a City*, 187.
28. Welsh, *Tanning in the United States*, 15.
29. Russell H. Austin, *The Milwaukee Story* (Milwaukee, WI: The Journal Company, 1946).
30. *The Century Club of Business in Milwaukee* Reprinted from the *Milwaukee Sentinel* (Milwaukee, WI: The

Journal Company, 1966), 28–29.

31. Still, *Milwaukee: The History of a City*, 188.

34. "Albert Trostel & Sons," 3.

Chapter Two

1. *Successful American*, 754.
2. Still, *Milwaukee: The History of a City*, 192.
3. Langill and Jensen, *Milwaukee 150*, 32.
4. "Albert Trostel & Sons," 3.
5. Ibid.
6. Robert W. Wells, *This is Milwaukee* (Milwaukee, WI: Renaissance Books, 1970), 124.
7. "Albert Trostel & Sons," 3.
8. Austin, *The Milwaukee Story*.
9. "Albert Trostel & Sons," 114.
10. Still, *Milwaukee: The History of a City*, 256.
11. Ibid., 201.
12. Wells, *This is Milwaukee*, 116.
13. Wells, *Yesterday's Milwaukee*, 34–5.
14. Wells, *This is Milwaukee*, 124.
15. Ibid.
16. Ibid.
17. Andrew J. Aikens and Lewis A. Proctor, *Men of Progress, Wisconsin* (Milwaukee, WI: The Evening Wisconsin Co., 1897), 257.
18. "Albert Trostel & Sons," 3.
19. Still, *Milwaukee: The History of a City*, 334.

20. John G. Gregory, *History of Milwaukee, WI* (The SJ Clarke Publishing Co, 1931), 536.
21. Ibid.
22. John Gurda, *The Making of Milwaukee* (Brookfield, WI: Burton and Mayer Inc., 1999), 120.
23. Gregory, *History of Milwaukee, WI*, 536.
24. Gurda, *The Making of Milwaukee*, 120.
25. George J. Lankevich, ed. *Milwaukee: A Chronological and Documentary History 1673–1977* (Dobbs Ferry, NY: Oceana Publications Inc., 1977), 44.
26. Still, *Milwaukee: The History of a City*, 324.
27. Ibid., 335.
28. Gurda, *The Making of Milwaukee*, 161.
29. Still, *Milwaukee: The History of a City*, 335.
30. Ibid., 257–8.
31. Ibid., 259–60.
32. Lankevich, *Milwaukee: A Chronological and Documentary History*, 44.
33. Ibid.
34. Ibid., 113.
35. *Remember When* (Milwaukee Public Library, 1973), 13.
36. Lankevich, *Milwaukee: A Chronological and Documentary History*, 111.
37. Ibid., 112.

38. Frank Abial Flower, *History of Milwaukee 1854–1911*, 1440.
39. Ibid.
40. W. G. Bruce, *History of Milwaukee*, 1922, (photocopy from Albert Trostel & Sons company archives).
41. Aikens and Proctor, *Men of Progress*, 258.
42. *Successful American*, 754.
43. Gallun Family Tree, Albert Trostel & Sons company archives.
44. *The Industrial History of Milwaukee, 1886*, (photocopy from Albert Trostel & Sons company archives), 96.
45. Ibid.
46. Ibid.
47. Ibid.
48. "Albert Trostel & Sons," 3.
49. *The Industrial History of Milwaukee, 1886*, 96.
50. Ibid.
51. Henry Eskuche, "Leather and the Tanning Industry," *Milwaukee's Great Industries*, William J. Anderson and Julius Bleyer, eds. (Milwaukee, WI: Association for the Advancement of Milwaukee, 1892), 225.
52. Ibid., 158.
53. "Albert Trostel & Sons," 3.
54. Aikens and Proctor, *Men of Progress*, 258.

Chapter Two Sidebar:
Making Leather

1. Lucille Preuss, "Romance in Leather," *Milwaukee Journal*, 20 April 1955.
2. Ibid.
3. Ibid.
4. Ibid.
5. Ibid.
6. Ibid.
7. Ibid.
8. *World Book Encyclopedia*, 1984 ed., s.v. "Leather."
9. Preuss, "Romance in Leather."
10. Ibid.
11. *World Book Encyclopedia.*
12. Preuss, "Romance in Leather."
13. *World Book Encyclopedia.*
14. Preuss, "Romance in Leather."
15. Ibid.
16. Ibid.
17. Ibid.
18. Ibid.

Chapter Three

1. Eskuche, "Leather and the Tanning Industry," 157.
2. Ibid., 158.
3. *Successful American*, 794.
4. Ibid.
5. Lankevich, *Milwaukee: A Chronological and Documentary History*, 48.
6. Ibid., 114.
7. Ibid.

8. Gallun Family Tree.
9. *Lower East Side Neighborhood History Resources Survey* s.v. "Albert Trostel" (City of Milwaukee, 1988), 478.
10. Ibid., 476.
11. Ibid., 478.
12. Still, *Milwaukee: The History of a City*, 122.
13. *Milwaukee Sentinel*, 18 May 1983.
14. "Albert Trostel & Sons Company History," photocopy, Albert Trostel & Sons company archives.
15. Ibid.
16. *Lower East Side Neighborhood Survey*, 476–8.
17. Ibid., 478.
18. *Illustrated Description of Milwaukee* (Milwaukee, WI: Daily Sentinel, 1889), 133.
19. Lankevich, *Milwaukee: A Chronological and Documentary History*, 49.
20. *Successful American*, 754.
21. "Albert Trostel & Sons."
22. *The Book of Milwaukee*, 1901, 4.
23. Ibid.
24. Still, *Milwaukee: The History of a City*, 342.
25. Langill and Jensen, *Milwaukee 150*, 49.
26. Still, *Milwaukee: The History of a City*, 494–5.
27. *The Book of Milwaukee*, 4.
28. Wells, *This is Milwaukee*, 148–51.

29. Lankevich, *Milwaukee: A Chronological and Documentary History*, 112.
30. Trostel Family Tree.
31. Russell H. Zimmermann, *Magnificent Milwaukee: Architectural Treasures, 1850–1920* (Menomonee Falls: Inland Press, 1987), 153.
32. Trostel Family Tree.
33. Shirley McArthur, *Northpoint Historic Districts, Milwaukee: An Architectural & Historical Inventory* (Milwaukee, WI: Northpoint Historical Society, 1981), 112.
34. Zimmermann, *Magnificent Milwaukee*, 153.
35. Joseph J. Korom, *Milwaukee Architecture: A Guide to Notable Buildings* (Madison, WI: Prairie Oak Press, 1995), 174.
36. Ibid., 155.
37. Zimmermann, *Magnificent Milwaukee*, 157.
38. Ibid.
39. Ibid.
40. Ibid., 155.
41. Wells, *This is Milwaukee*, 105.
42. Ibid.
43. Ibid., 105–07.
44. Trostel Family Tree.
45. *Milwaukee Sentinel*, 8 May 1983.
46. Karom, *Milwaukee Architecture*, 187.

47. *Milwaukee Journal*, 1 May 1936.
48. Ibid.
49. *Milwaukee Sentinel*, 18 May 1983.
50. Ibid.
51. Albert Trostel & Sons company archives.
52. *Successful American*, 754.
53. Wells, *This is Milwaukee*, 182.
54. "Charity Bazar March 2 to 7, 1916," Wisconsin, Wohltatigkeits-Basar program, 29.
55. Lankevich, *Milwaukee: A Chronological and Documentary History*, 58.
56. Gurda, *Making of Milwaukee*, 240.
57. "Albert Trostel & Sons," 4.
58. McArthur, *Northpoint Historic Districts, Milwaukee*, 112.

Chapter Four

1. Still, *Milwaukee: The History of a City*, 477.
2. Ibid.
3. Ibid., 478.
4. Ibid.
5. Ibid.
6. Ibid.
7. Ibid.
8. Wells, *This is Milwaukee*, 211.
9. Still, *Milwaukee: The History of a City*, 478.
10. Wells, *This is Milwaukee*, 212.
11. Wells, *Yesterday's Milwaukee*, 114.
12. Ibid., 117.
13. *Milwaukee Sentinel*, 14 January 1965.
14. Albert Trostel & Sons, minutes of board of directors meeting, 29 January 1932.
15. Albert Trostel & Sons, minutes of board of directors meeting, 19 March 1932.
16. Albert Trostel & Sons, minutes of board of directors meeting, 31 March 1932, 2.
17. Ibid.
18. Ibid., 2–3.
19. Ibid., 3.
20. Ibid., 2–3.
21. Ibid., 5.
22. Ibid., 1–2.
23. Albert Trostel & Sons, minutes of board of directors meeting, 28 July 1932.
24. Albert Trostel & Sons, minutes of board of directors meeting, 1 November 1932.
25. Albert Trostel & Sons, minutes of board of directors meeting, 6 January 1933, 2.
26. Ibid.
27. Probate Records, Milwaukee Historical Society.
28. *Milwaukee Journal*, 2 October 1956.
29. *Milwaukee Sentinel*, 11 May 1983.
30. Ibid.
31. Albert Trostel & Sons, minutes of board of directors meeting, 6 January 1933.
32. Albert Trostel & Sons, minutes of board of directors meeting, 18 January 1933.
33. Special meeting of stockholders, Albert Trostel & Sons, 31 March 1932, 1–2.
34. Stockholders Annual Meeting, Albert Trostel & Sons, 8 February 1933, 2–15, 33.
35. Stockholders Annual Meeting, Albert Trostel & Sons, 17 February 1933.
36. Albert Trostel & Sons, minutes of board of directors meeting, 22 July 1933.
37. Special meeting of stockholders, Albert Trostel & Sons, 23 February 1934, 1.
38. Ibid., 1–2.
39. Special meeting of stockholders, Albert Trostel & Sons, 27 February 1934, 1–2.
40. Albert Trostel & Sons, minutes of board of directors meeting, 5 April 1934.
41. Albert Trostel & Sons, minutes of board of directors meeting, 23 December 1935.

42. Albert Trostel & Sons, minutes of board of directors meeting, 23 July 1936.

43. Albert Trostel & Sons, minutes of board of directors meeting, 17 October 1936.

44. Ibid.

45. Anders Segerdahl, interview by Jeffrey L. Rodengen, tape recording, 25 October 2002, Wrtie Stuff Enterprises.

46. Ibid.

47. *Trostelgram,* Milan, TN, 22 February 1962.

48. Segerdahl, interview.

49. Obituary, *Milwaukee Journal.*

50. *Milan Exchange.*

51. *Milwaukee Journal,* 2 February 1958.

52. Ibid.

53. Obituary.

54. *Business Ad Digest,* February, 1957.

55. Segerdahl, interview.

56. Obituary.

57. *Milan Exchange.*

58. *Business Ad Digest*

59. *Milan Exchange*

60. *Business Ad Digest.*

61. *Milan Exchange.*

62. Ibid.

Chapter Five

1. Langill and Jensen, *Milwaukee 150,* 85.

2. *Men of Achievement in Wisconsin* (Milwaukee, WI: John Moranz Assoc., 1946), 6.

3. Ibid., 5.

4. Ibid.

5. Ibid., 7.

6. Ibid., 5.

7. Langill & Jensen, *Milwaukee 150,* 85.

8. *Men of Achievement,* 6.

9. Ibid., 7.

10. Ibid., 6.

11. Ibid.

12. Deborah Trissel, "Albert Trostel & Sons," (company history, Albert Trostel & Sons company archives).

13. Albert Trostel & Sons, minutes of board of directors meeting, 14 October 1943.

14. Albert Trostel & Sons, minutes of board of directors meeting, 14 August 1941.

15. Albert Trostel & Sons, minutes of board of directors meeting, 10 December 1942.

16. Albert Trostel & Sons, minutes of board of directors meeting, 15 August 1941.

17. Frank Fermano, interview by Jeffrey L. Rodengen, tape recording, 23 September 2002, Write Stuff Enterprises.

18. Ibid.

19. Ibid.

20. Albert Trostel & Sons, minutes of board of directors meeting, 16 April 1942.

21. "Industry-Wide Readjustments Made in Second Full Year of War," (Hide and Leather Publishing Co., 1944, photocopy, Albert Trostel & Sons company archives).

22. Ibid.

23. Ibid.

24. Albert Trostel & Sons, minutes of board of directors meeting, 1 October 1943.

25. Albert Trostel & Sons, minutes of board of directors meeting, 1 August 1944.

26. Albert Trostel & Sons, minutes of board of directors meetings, 29 June 1945, July 1946, 30 June 1947, 6 June 1948.

27. Albert Trostel & Sons, minutes of board of directors meeting, 16 November 1944.

28. Ibid.

29. Albert Trostel & Sons, minutes of board of directors meeting, 18 December 1946.

30. Albert Trostel & Sons, minutes of board of directors meetings, 21

December 1945, 18
December 1946, 20
December 1948.

31. Albert Trostel & Sons,
minutes of board of
directors meeting, 25 April
1944.

32. Albert Trostel & Sons,
minutes of board of
directors meetings, 18
December 1946, 17
December 1947, 20
December 1948.

33. Langill and Jensen,
Milwaukee 150, 86

34. *Men of Achievement*, 7.

35. Ibid., 8.

36. Ibid.

37. Langill and Jensen,
Milwaukee 150, 90.

38. *Men of Achievement*, 8.

39. Albert Trostel & Sons,
minutes of board of
directors meeting, 17
December 1947.

40. Ibid.

41. Fermano, interview.

42. Ibid.

43. Albert Trostel & Sons,
minutes of board of
directors meeting, 26 April
1948.

Chapter Six

1. *Blue Book History*, Albert
Trostel & Sons company
archives, 8.

2. Fermano, interview.

3. *Blue Book*, 8.

4. Fermano, interview.

5. *Albert Trostel & Sons Company:
A Profile*, Albert Trostel &
Sons company archives, 1
December 1972.

6. *Blue Book*, 10.

7. Ibid.

8. Bessie Bradwell Helmer,
"The Great Conflagration,"
Chicago Historical Society
and Northwestern University,
www.chicagohs.org/fire, 8
October 1996.

9. *Blue Book*, 10.

10. Langill & Jensen,
Milwaukee 150, 88–9.

11. Ibid.

12. *Blue Book*, 14.

13. Ibid.

14. Albert Trostel & Sons
company archives.

15. Ibid.

16. Ibid.

17. Fermano, interview.

18. Robert Gamache, interview
by Jeffrey L. Rodengen,
tape recording, 24
September 2002, Write
Stuff Enterprises.

19. Trostel Polymer
Compounding Division,
"Trostel PCD Profile,"
www.trostelpcd.com/
aboutpcd.htm.

20. Merrill Karcher, interview
by Richard F. Hubbard, tape
recording, 25 October 2002,
Write Stuff Enterprises.

21. Albert Trostel & Sons
company archives.

22. Ibid.

23. Ibid.

24. Ibid.

25. *Milwaukee Journal*, 10
February 1956.

26. Albert Trostel & Sons,
minutes of board of
directors meeting, 1956.

27. Smedal, "Trostel
Company: One of
America's Tannery
Titans," *Milwaukee
Sentinel*, 1958.

28. Ibid.

29. Albert O. Trostel III,
interview by Richard
F. Hubbard, tape
recording, 21 October 2002,
Write Stuff Enterprises.

30. Smedal, "Trostel Company:
One of America's Tannery
Titans."

31. Ibid.

32. Charles Koch, interview
by Richard F. Hubbard,
tape recording, 30
October 2002, Write
Stuff Enterprises.

33. Smedal, "Trostel Company:
One of America's Tannery
Titans."

34. Ibid.

35. Segerdahl, interview.

36. Smedal, "Trostel Company:
One of America's Tannery
Titans."

37. Albert Trostel & Sons,
minutes of board of
directors meeting, 1951,
1953.

38. Albert Trostel & Sons, minutes of board of directors meeting, 1954, 1955.
39. *Milwaukee Journal,* 2 February 1958.
40. *Milwaukee Journal,* 16 February 1958.
41. *Milwaukee Journal,* 16 February 1958.
42. Ibid.
43. *Milwaukee Journal,* February 1958.
44. *Jackson Sun,* 25 January 2001.
45. Segerdahl, interview.
46. Ibid.
47. Ibid.
48. *Memphis Press-Scimitar,* 27 January 1961.
49. *Jackson Sun,* January 1961.
50. *Memphis Press-Scimitar,* 27 January 1961.
51. Segerdahl, interview.
52. Ibid.
53. Ibid.
54. Albert O. Trostel III, interview.
55. Albert Trostel & Sons, minutes of board of directors meeting, 19 February 1962.
56. Ibid.
57. Ibid.
58. Fermano, interview.
59. Frank Gotlein, *Milwaukee Journal,* 2 February 1958.

Chapter Six Sidebar:
The Art World Responds

1. Gotlein, *Milwaukee Journal.*

Chapter Six Sidebar:
One Hundred Years of Globalism, Progressivism, and Traditionalism

1. Thomas L. Friedman, *The Lexus and the Olive Tree* (New York: Random House, 2000), xvii.

Chapter Seven

1. Segerdahl, interview.
2. Ibid.
3. Karcher, interview.
4. Ibid.
5. Fermano, interview.
6. Ibid.
7. Ibid.
8. Fermano, interview.
9. Albert O. Trostel III, interview.
10. Julian Hatton Jr., interview by Jeffrey L. Rodengen, tape recording, 23 September 2002, Write Stuff Enterprises.
11. Ibid.
12. Ibid.
13. Albert Trostel & Sons, minutes of board of directors meeting, 31 October 1966.
14. Hatton, interview.
15. Charles Krull, interview by Richard F. Hubbard, tape recording, 11 December 2002, Write Stuff Enterprises.
16. "Albert Trostel & Sons," company history, Albert Trostel & Sons company archives.
17. Krull, interview.
18. "Albert Trostel & Sons," company history, Albert Trostel & Sons company archives.
19. Ibid.
20. Ibid.
21. Krull, interview.
22. "Albert Trostel & Sons," company history, Albert Trostel & Sons company archives.
23. Krull, interview.
24. Albert O. Trostel III, interview.
25. Ibid.
26. Krull, interview.

Chapter Seven Sidebar:
The History of Eagle Ottawa

1. *Muskegon Chronicle,* 9 July 1985.
2. Eagle Tanning Works, minutes of board of directors meeting, 7 January 1896.
3. *Muskegon Chronicle.*
4. Ibid.
5. Hatton, interview.
6. *Muskegon Chronicle.*
7. Ibid.
8. Ibid.
9. Hatton, interview.

10. Ibid.
11. Eagle Ottawa Company, minutes of board of directors meeting, 26 May 1961.
12. Hatton, interview.
13. Ibid.
14. *Muskegon Chronicle.*

**Chapter Seven Sidebar:
Everett G. Smith: A Profile**

1. Everett Smith Group Ltd., timeline.
2. Segerdahl, interview.
3. *Trostelgram,* 22 February 1962.
4. Tom Hauske Jr., interview by Jeffrey L. Rodengen, tape recording, 26 July 2002, Write Stuff Enterprises.
5. Randy Perry, interview by Jeffrey L. Rodengen, tape recording, 15 October 2003.
6. Fermano, interview.
7. *Trostelgram,* 22 February 1962.
8. Anita Hauske, interview by Jeffrey L. Rodengen, tape recording, 19 December 2002, Write Stuff Enterprises.
9. Ibid.
10. Tom Hauske Jr., interview.
11. Ibid.

Chapter Eight

1. "Albert Trostel & Sons," company history, Albert

Trostel & Sons company archives.
2. Tom Hauske Jr., interview.
3. Segerdahl, interview.
4. Krull, interview.
5. Segerdahl, interview.
6. Ibid.
7. Ibid.
8. *Blue Book.*
9. Segerdahl, interview.
10. Albert O. Trostel III, interview.
11. Nancy Schlicher, interview by Richard F. Hubbard, tape recording, 21 October 2002, Write Stuff Enterprises.
12. Joyce Huck, interview by Richard F. Hubbard, tape recording, 23 September 2002.
13. Ibid.
14. Gamache, interview.
15. Ibid.
16. Huck, interview.
17. Ibid.
18. Gamache, interview.
19. Ibid.
20. Anders Segerdahl, interview.
21. Jim Orth, interview by Richard F. Hubbard, tape recording, 12 March 2002.
22. Ibid.
23. Segerdahl, interview.
24. Ibid.
25. Ibid.
26. Ibid.
27. Ibid.
28. Ibid.
29. Ibid.
30. Ibid.

31. Gamache, interview.
32. Ibid.
33. Fermano, interview.
34. Gamache, interview.
35. Ibid.
36. Huck, interview.
37. Karcher, interview.
38. Gamache, interview.
39. Tim Baker, interview by Jeffrey L. Rodengen, tape recording, 1 October 2002, Write Stuff Enterprises.
40. Ibid.
41. Gamache, interview.

**Chapter Eight Sidebar:
Anders Segerdahl: A Profile**

1. "Anders Segerdahl Profile," Albert Trostel & Sons company archives.
2. Segerdahl, interview.
3. Ibid.
4. Ibid.
5. "Anders Segerdahl Profile,"
6. Segerdahl, interview.
7. Ibid.
8. Ibid.
9. Ibid.
10. Ibid.
11. Ibid.
12. Ibid.
13. Ibid
14. Ibid.
15. Ibid.
16. Ibid.
17. Ibid.
18. Ibid.
19. Ibid.

20. Ibid.
21. Ibid.
22. Ibid.
23. Ibid.

Chapter Eight Sidebar:
Eagle Ottawa Process

1. Helmut Beutel, interview by Richard F. Hubbard, tape recording, 29 October 2002, Write Stuff Enterprises.
2. Ibid.
3. Ibid.
4. Ibid.
5. Ibid.
6. Ibid.
7. Ibid.
8. Pat Oldenkamp, interview by Richard F. Hubbard, tape recording, 25 November 2002, Write Stuff Enterprises.
9. Beutel, interview.

Chapter Nine

1. Perry, interview, 26 July 2002.
2. Ibid.
3. Ibid.
4. Ibid.
5. Ibid.
6. Ibid.
7. Ibid.
8. Segerdahl, interview.
9. Tom Hauske Jr., interview.
10. Segerdahl, interview.
11. Ibid.
12. Eagle Ottawa Leather Ltd., company profile, 2.

13. Neil Dunn, interview by Richard F. Hubbard, tape recording, 11 October 2002.
14. Segerdahl, interview.
15. Dunn, interview.
16. Oldenkamp, interview.
17. Baker, interview.
18. Ibid.
19. Ibid.
20. Huck, interview.
21. Ibid.
22. Ibid.
23. Dunn, interview.
24. Segerdahl, interview.
25. Randy Perry, interview by Jon VanZile, tape recording, 15 October 2003, Write Stuff Enterprises.
26. Ibid.
27. Tom Hauske Jr., interview.
28. Ibid.
29. Ibid.
30. Ibid.
31. Ibid.
32. Perry, interview, 26 July 2002.
33. Jerry Sumpter, interview by Richard F. Hubbard, tape recording, 25 October 2002, Write Stuff Enterprises.
34. Perry, interview, 26 July 2002.
35. Craig Tonti, interview by Richard F. Hubbard, tape recording, 24 October 2002, Write Stuff Enterprises.
36. Sumpter, interview.
37. Tom Hauske Jr., interview.
38. Gamache, interview.

39. Ibid.
40. Ibid.
41. Thomas Mahnke, interview by Richard F. Hubbard, tape recording, 8 October 2002, Write Stuff Enterprises.
42. "Albert Trostel & Sons," company history, Albert Trostel & Sons company archives.
43. Michael Kirst, interview by Richard F. Hubbard, tape recording, 23 October 2002, Write Stuff Enterprises.
44. "Albert Trostel & Sons," company history, Albert Trostel & Sons company archives.
45. Kirst, interview.
46. "Albert Trostel & Sons," company history, Albert Trostel & Sons company archives.

Chapter Nine Sidebar:
Greener Pastures

1. "Eagle Ottawa Story," company archives.
2. Ibid.
3. Ibid.
4. Beutel, interview.
5. "Eagle Ottawa Story."
6. Ibid.
7. Ibid.
8. Ibid.
9. Eagle Ottawa Leather Ltd., company profile, 22.

10. Eagle Ottawa Leather Company, "Newaygo Farms—The First Step in Quality," Eagle Ottawa LLC, www.eagleottawa.com/environment/newaygo.html.
11. "Eagle Ottawa Story."
12. Tonti, interview.

Chapter Ten

1. Sumpter, interview.
2. Perry, interview, 26 July 2002.
3. Gamache, interview.
4. Ibid.
5. Ibid.
6. Bruce Betters, interview by Richard F. Hubbard, tape recording, 11 October 2002, Write Stuff Enterprises.
7. DeWayne Egly, interview by Jeffrey L. Rodengen, tape recording, 27 September 2002, Write Stuff Enterprises.
8. Gamache, interview.
9. Egly, interview.
10. Ibid.
11. Ibid.
12. Ibid.
13. Gamache, interview.
14. Charlie Hicks, interview by Richard F. Hubbard, tape recording, 1 November 2002, Write Stuff Enterprises.

15. Thomas Sloane, interview by Richard F. Hubbard, tape recording, 10 October 2002, Write Stuff Enterprises.
16. Kirst, interview.
17. Sloane, interview.
18. Ibid.
19. Ibid.
20. Kirst, interview.
21. Ibid.
22. Dunn, interview.
23. Randy Perry, interview by Jeffrey L. Rodengen and Torey Marcus, tape recording, 9 December 2003, Write Stuff Enterprises.
24. Dunn, interview.
25. Perry, interview, 26 July 2002.
26. Ibid.
27. Information supplied by Albert Trostel & Sons to Torey Marcus, 8 March 2004.
28. Kevin Velik, interview by Richard F. Hubbard, tape recording, 29 October 2002, Write Stuff Enterprises.
29. Ibid.
30. Betters, interview.
31. Perry, interview, 26 July 2002.
32. Perry, interview, 9 December 2003.
33. Patrick Roeser, interview by Richard F. Hubbard, tape

recording, 15 October 2002, Write Stuff Enterprises.
34. Information supplied by Albert Trostel & Sons to Torey Marcus, 8 March 2004.
35. Perry, interview, 26 July 2002.
36. Ibid.
37. Orth, interview.
38. Perry, interview, 26 July 2002.
39. Perry, interview, 15 October 2003.
40. "Trostel SEG Acquires Techniplas, Inc.," Trostel SEG, www.trostelseg.com/whatsnewpage.html.
41. Ibid.
42. Ibid.
43. Sloane, interview.
44. Ibid.
45. Betters, interview.
46. Perry, interview, 15 October 2003.
47. Egly, interview.
48. Sumpter, interview.
49. Tonti, interview.
50. Perry, interview, 26 July 2002.
51. Sumpter, interview.
52. Thomas Mahnke, interview.
53. Information supplied by Albert Trostel & Sons to Torey Marcus, 8 March 2004.
54. Segerdahl, interview.

INDEX

Page numbers in italics indicate photographs.

A

A. F. Gallun & Sons, 63
acquisitions and mergers
    Berman facility, 92
    Callow & Maddox,
        99–100
    Eagle Ottawa, 68, 74–75
    Pierpoint & Bryant, 92
    Techniplas Inc.,
        122–123
advertising, 32, 33
Albert O. Trostel
    Foundation, 51
Albert Trostel Packings
    Ltd., *94. See also*
    Polyurethane
    Division; Trostel Ltd.
    customer service, 93–94
    leather seals, 71–72
    origin of, 55, 57–60
    production technology,
        89
    restructuring, 104, 106
    transition to rubber and
        synthetics, 93, 101

Allen, Rufus, 16, 21
Allis, Edward P., 16
Allis Chalmers, 37
American Hair & Felt Co.,
    62
art collection, *10, 18, 30,*
    38, 46, 54, 63,
    63–65, 64, 70, 82,
    96, 112
Audi, 118
automotive industry, 55,
    84–85. *See also* Eagle
    Ottawa Leather Co.
automotive upholstery, *80,*
    84, 100
awards, *98, 102–103, 103,*
    107

B

B. B. Walker, 87
Badger Meter, 79
Baker, Tim, 94–95, 101
Bean, Cary, 119
Bendix, 83
Berman family, 92

Betters, Bruce, 114, 123
Beutel, Helmut, 90
Blanchard Brother and
    Lane, 68, 74
BMW, 118
Boggs, Franklin, 63. *See*
    also art collection
Bosch, 101, 111
Bradley and Metcalf, 23,
    33
Breedlove, Craig, 71
Briggs & Stratton, 93, 117
Brown Shoe Co., 87
Business of the Year
    award, *98*

C

cafeteria, *65*
Callow & Maddox, *98, 99,*
    99–100
cast urethane applications,
    117
Chase Manhattan Bank, 40
Chrysler, 85, 91
corporate culture, 67

Corsi, George, *88*
Crown Corp., 117
Curtiembres Fonseca, 113
Curtiembres Tarud
          Limitada, 51

D

Delphi, 101
Dunn, Neil, *99*, 99–100,
          101, 104, 118
DuPont, 94

E

Eagle Ottawa de Mexico
          S.A. de C.V., 98–99
Eagle Ottawa Fonseca, 113
Eagle Ottawa Leather Co.,
          *73, 75, 83, 92, 99,
          110*
     acquisition by Trostel, 68
     automotive industry
          and, 83–85, 91–92
     changing technology,
          72–73
     cutting and sewing
          operations, 98–101
     future of, 123–125
     history, *74–75*
     international expansion,
          98–101, 101, 104,
          113, *113*, 117–120,
          119
     Jerry Sumpter,
          recruitment of,
          107–108
     tanning process, *90*,
          90–91
Eagle Ottawa Leather Ltd.,
          98–99

Eagle Ottawa South Africa,
          101, 104, *108–109*,
          118, *118*
Eagle Tanning Co., 92–93
"E" award, 51, *51*
ECA Otero HNOS, 86
Edgar Ricker & Co., 78
Egly, DeWayne, *114*,
          114–115, 123
Empire Tannery, 22, 28
environmentalism,
          102–103
Everett Smith Investments,
          83, 97, 104

F

F. Mayer Boot and Shoe
          Co., 33
Falk, Cutler Hammer, 37
Fermano, Frank, *88*
     on Albert O. Trostel Jr.,
          69
     on Everett Smith, 79
     postwar strategy, 53
     retirement, 93
     Trostel Packings, 71–72,
          88
     war production, 50
financial performance
     1940s, 51, 53
     1950s, 58, 62
     1960s, 80
     2002-2003, 122, 123
Finkler, Adolph, 34, 36, 40,
          43
Finkler, Albert Trostel, 34
Finkler, Charlotte, 34
Finkler, Ida Trostel, 28, 34,
          36, 40
fires, 19, *22*, 22–23, 42

First Wisconsin, 79
Ford Motor Co., 85, 91, *123*
furniture upholstery, 71

G

Gallun, Albert F., 27, 28,
          28
Gallun, Arthur H. Edwin,
          27
Gallun, August, 19–28, 27
Gallun, Edwin A., 27
Gallun, Ella, 27
Gallun, Julia Kraus, 27
Gamache, Bob, 89
     on Frank Fermano, 93
     Mexico expansion,
          108–110, 113–114
     retirement, 114
     technology at Trostel
          Packings, 89
Gao, Dinggui, *119*
General Motors, 85, 91, 101
General Shoe Corp., 74
Genesco Inc., 80, 87
Getlein, Frank, 64, 65
Gould, David, *102*
*Grand Haven Daily
          Tribune*, 69
Grand Haven Leather Co.,
          74
Great Depression, 39–45
Grimes, Tom, 123

H

Harley Davidson, 37
Hatton, Julian, 74
Hatton, Julian B. Jr., 73,
          74, 81
Hatton, William, 74

Hauske, Anita Smith, 79
Hauske, Tom Jr., 79,
    98, 104, *106*, 107,
    108
H. H. Brown, 87
Hicks, Charlie, 115–116
Huck, Joyce, 88, 89, 93,
    101

I

Illinois Leather Co., 36
incorporation, 36
international expansion
    Argentina, 113
    China, *119*, 119–120
    Colombia, 51
    Hungary, *113*, 117–118
    Mexico, 98, 108–110,
        113–114, 118
    South Africa, 101, 104,
        108–109, 118, *118*
    United Kingdom,
        99–100

K

Karcher, Merrill, *94*
    on customer service,
        94
    joins Trostel Packings,
        58
    on seals, 71–72
    Trostel Packings, 89
Kefauver, Estes, 67
Kirst, Michael, 111, 116,
    117
Koch, Charles, 60
Krug, August, 35
Krull, Charles, 76, 79, 80,
    84, 89

Kuechel, Karl, 45

L

labor unions, 57
Lake Geneva, Wis., 55–57
Liebert, Eugene, 35, 36
Liebert, Hans, 35
Lines, Spooner and
    Quarles, 40, 43
logo, *97*

M

Mahnke, Thomas, 110, 125
Marshall Street office, *125*
Mattel Corp., 79
Mazda, 118
Metz Leather, 74
Midwest Oil & Protein Co.,
    83
Milan, Tenn., plant, 66–67
Milwaukee
    brewing industry,
        14–15
    German immigration to,
        13–14
    Great Depression,
        effects of, 39
    history, 11–17, *12*, *14*,
        20, 20–21, 24–26
    homes, *31*, 34–35
    meat industry, 15
    social clubs, 36, 44
    tanning industry,
        15–17, *16*
    World War I, 36–37
    World War II, 47, 49,
        51, 53
Milwaukee Blood Center,
    79
Milwaukee Brewers, 79

Milwaukee Hide and
    Leather Co., 22–23
Milwaukee Lace Paper, 43
Milwaukee tannery, *65*, 73,
    76, *76–77*, 80–81

N

New York Tanners Council,
    65
Nichol, Anderson, 53
Northwestern Mutual Life
    Insurance Co., 41, 79
Notz, Elinor Trostel, 36
Notz, John, 36

O

offal, 60
Oldenkamp, Pat, 91,
    100–101
Old Paper Mill property, 22
100th anniversary, 62–63,
    63
Orth, Jim, 91–92, 121
Ottawa Leather Co., 74

P

Perry, Randy, *118*, *120*
    on Anders Segerdahl, 107
    Argentina joint venture,
        113
    on China, 119
    on Everett Smith, 79
    on future of Albert
        Trostel & Sons,
        122–125
    on Hungarian plant, 118
    positions at Trostel, 97,
        106, 120

Pfister, Guido, 17, 21
Pfister and Vogel tannery, 29
Phoenix leather, 102
Phoenix Tannery, 23, *23*, 28, 32, 55
Pierpoint & Bryant, 92, 99
Pipkorn, Frank A., 42
Polymer Compounding Division, 58
Polyurethane Division, 58, 93–94, 95, 97–98
production, streamlining of, 59–60
purses, *47*

R

Range Rover, 118
Raymond Corp., 117
Read, Erna Trostel, 34, 40
research and development, 94
Roeser, Patrick, 119–120

S

Schlicher, Nancy, 88
Schlitz family and brewery, 14–15, *15*, 35–36, 79
Schroeder, William, 17
seals and packings, 55, *68*, 71–72, *72*, *122*
Segerdahl, Anders, 85, *102*, *124*
    on Eagle Ottawa acquisition, 68
    environmentalism, *102*, 102–103
    Everett Smith, death of, 107

on future of Albert Trostel & Sons, 125
    leadership, 120–121
    ownership interest, 83
    president of Eagle Ottawa, 75, 81
    profile, 86–87
    tanneries acquistions, 92–93
    on tanning industry, 65–66
Segerdahl, Birgit, 86–87
Selig, Bud, 79
shoes, *48*, *52*
Sloane, Thomas, 116–117, *122*, 123
Smith, Everett G., *44*, *63*
    death, 106–107
    joins Trostel, 44
    leadership, 62, 120–121
    named president, 68–69
    ownership interest, 83, 97, 104
    profile, *78*, 78–79
    tanneries acquistions, 93
    on tannery closing, 80
Smith, Gertrude Kasten, 79
Snap On Tools, 117
Sproule, Ilse Trostel, 34, 40
Star Tannery, 19, 28, 32
Strackbein, John, 57, 71
Strattec, 117
Sulm, Roman, 21
Sumpter, Jerry, 107–108, 113, *120*, 123, 125

T

tanneries (Trostel plants)
    Empire Tannery, 22, 28

Milwaukee, *65*, 73, 76, *76–77*, 80–81
Phoenix Tannery, 23, *23*, 28, 32, *55*
Pierpoint & Bryant, 92, 99
Star Tannery, 19, 28, 32
Trostel and Gallun tannery, *19*, 19–28, *20–21*
Waterloo, Iowa, 91–92
tanning process, 24–27, 90–91, 102–103
Texas Boot, 87
Theodore Roosevelt Conservation Award, 103, *103*
Tonti, Craig, 103, 108, 124
Town & Country shoes, *48*
Toyota Superior Quality Award, 107, *107*
Trostan calf, 37
Trostel, Albert Gottlieb, *11*, 13, 17, 19–28, 32
Trostel, Albert O., 28, *31*, 32, 34–36, 40–43
Trostel, Albert O. III, 58, 72, 80, 88
Trostel, Albert O. Jr., 39
    birth, 36
    on Clara Trostel, 58
    death, 68–69
    on Eagle acquisition, 75
    family, 58
    leadership, 42–45, 58
    succeeds father as president, 41
    World War II, 49–53
Trostel, Andreas, 13
Trostel, Anna W. Bossert, 34

Trostel, Charlotte, 28, 32
Trostel, Clara Louise, 58
Trostel, Clara Uihlein
    Anders Segerdahl and,
        86
    death, 58
    Everett Smith,
        recruitment of, 78
    family, 35, 35
    home, 41
    loans and influence on
        company, 40, 42–44
Trostel, Georg Michael, 13
Trostel, Gustav
    birth, 28
    community activities, 36
    death, 43
    Depression years, 40,
        42–43
    family home, 31, 34–35
    named president, 36
    training as tanner, 32
Trostel, Jacobus, 13
Trostel, Janet Orr, 58
Trostel, Kendrick, 58
Trostel, Otto A. (son of
        Gustav), 34, 40
Trostel, Otto (son of Albert),
        28, 43
Trostel, Tara Kendrick,
        58

Trostel and Gallun tannery,
        19, 19–28, 20, 21
Trostel Aviation, 62, 62, 83
Trostel Compounding Ltd.,
        83
Trostel-Gallun family
        conflict, 28
Trostel Industries Inc., 83
Trostel Ltd., 105, 115, 122,
        124
    Mexico, expansion in,
        108–110, 113
    name change, 106
Trostel SEG and, 123
Trostel Mechanical
        Industries Inc., 83
Trostel SEG, 104, 106,
        111, 116, 117, 121
    expansion, 116–117
    origin of, 106
    polyurethane
        technology, 110–111
Trostel Ltd. and, 123
Trostel Tool and Die, 83
Trostel Trading Co., 83

U-V

Uihlein, Edgar, 58
Uihlein family, 35–36
United States Glue Co., 36

Vamac, 94, 101
Velik, Kevin, 118
Vogel, Frederick, 17, 21
Volkswagen, 118
Volvo, 118

W

Waterloo, Iowa, tannery,
        91–92
Weicker, Beatrice Trostel,
        36
Weicker, Frederick, 36
Weiler, Anna Marie, 13
Weinbrenner, 87
Western Leather Co., 36
Western Publishing, 79
Weyenberg Shoe
        Manufacturing Co.,
        33
Whirlpool Corp., 83
Whitewater, Wis., plant, 94,
        101
Wisconsin Leather Co., 21
World War I, 36–37
World War II, 49–53, 50, 53

Z

Zeidler, Frank, 65
Zohrlaut, Herman, 21